ASIAN POLITICAL, ECONOMIC AND SECURITY ISSUES

VIETNAM

SERVICE SECTOR GROWTH

ASIAN POLITICAL, ECONOMIC AND SECURITY ISSUES

Additional books in this series can be found on Nova's website under the Series tab.

Additional E-books in this series can be found on Nova's website under the E-book tab.

ASIAN POLITICAL, ECONOMIC AND SECURITY ISSUES

VIETNAM

SERVICE SECTOR GROWTH

RHETT R. MURPHY
EDITOR

nova publishers
New York

For permission to use material from this book please contact us:
Telephone 631-231-7269; Fax 631-231-8175
Web Site: http://www.novapublishers.com

Library of Congress Cataloging-in-Publication Data

ISBN: 978-1-62417-549-7

Published by Nova Science Publishers, Inc. † New York

CONTENTS

PREFACE

This book provides an overview and examination of the Vietnamese services sector. Vietnam is growing rapidly as it transitions from a state-planned economy to a hybrid economy with an expanded private sector. Besides broadening its international trade relationships, in recent years Vietnam has committed to liberalizing its industries and strengthening its intellectual property laws through bilateral treaties, regional associations, and accession to the World Trade Organization.

Service industries account for a growing share of Vietnam's economy, as new businesses seek services like banking and logistics while consumers with rising income demand education, retail, and telecommunication services.

Liberalization and foreign investment have increased the supply of services in Vietnam, but many industries are still hampered by shortages of skilled workers and good infrastructure, and by a weak business environment in which regulations impede commerce and state-owned enterprises have many advantages.

Chapter 1 – Vietnam is growing rapidly as it transitions from a state-planned economy to a hybrid economy with an expanded private sector. Besides broadening its international trade relationships, in recent years Vietnam has committed to liberalizing its industries and strengthening its intellectual property laws through bilateral treaties, regional associations, and accession to the World Trade Organization.

Service industries account for a growing share of Vietnam's economy, as new businesses seek services like banking and logistics while consumers with rising income demand education, retail, and telecommunication services.

Liberalization and foreign investment have increased the supply of services in Vietnam, but many industries are still hampered by shortages of skilled workers and good infrastructure, and by a weak business environment in which regulations impede commerce and state-owned enterprises have many advantages.

Chapter 2 – This is the Vietnam: Country Profile.

In: Vietnam: Service Sector Growth
Editor: Rhett R. Murphy
ISBN: 978-1-62417-549-7

Chapter 1

AN OVERVIEW AND EXAMINATION OF THE VIETNAMESE SERVICE SECTOR*

U.S. International Trade Commission

ABSTRACT

Vietnam is growing rapidly as it transitions from a state-planned economy to a hybrid economy with an expanded private sector. Besides broadening its international trade relationships, in recent years Vietnam has committed to liberalizing its industries and strengthening its intellectual property laws through bilateral treaties, regional associations, and accession to the World Trade Organization.

Service industries account for a growing share of Vietnam's economy, as new businesses seek services like banking and logistics while consumers with rising income demand education, retail, and telecommunication services.

Liberalization and foreign investment have increased the supply of services in Vietnam, but many industries are still hampered by shortages of skilled workers and good infrastructure, and by a weak business environment in which regulations impede commerce and state-owned enterprises have many advantages.

---

* This Working Paper was released by the U.S. International Trade Commission, Office of Industries, August 2012.

INTRODUCTION

Services are a vital part of Vietnam's plan to become a modern economy by 2020. The service sector is forecast to grow by 8–8.5 percent per year and to account for 42–43 percent of Vietnam's GDP during 2016–20,[1] and the Vietnamese government is implementing aggressive policies intended to accelerate the development of high-value-added services. Vietnam is increasing its presence in the global services market through its membership in the Association of Southeast Asian Nations (ASEAN) and through the commitments it made upon acceding to the World Trade Organization (WTO) in 2007. Vietnam also has a significant services trade relationship with the United States and is the recipient of increasing U.S. foreign direct investment (FDI), in part because the large Vietnamese American population in the United States provides economic and cultural ties.[2] Industry reforms and international integration are happening in the context of rapid growth after decades of war and political isolation, as the country is transitioning from a planned centralized economy to a hybrid economy (mixing private ownership and state influence) while maintaining one-party socialist governance.

This paper is the third in a series on service markets in emerging economies.[3] The balance of this introductory section examines supply and demand factors in the Vietnamese services market. The following section discusses Vietnam's services trade with the world. The paper then analyzes five key services industries in Vietnam: banking, education, logistics, retail, and telecommunications. The paper concludes with an examination of intellectual property rights in Vietnam, a cross-cutting issue affecting many services industries.

Overview of Services in Vietnam

In Vietnam, a lower-middle-income country with a population of 87 million, the service sector grew by 7.5 percent in 2010 and accounted for 38.3 percent of the country's $103 billion gross domestic product (GDP) that year.[4] In 2012, the service sector is forecast to grow by 6.2 percent, which surpasses agricultural growth (3.0 percent) but lags slightly behind forecasted growth in manufacturing (6.5 percent).[5] The number of registered enterprises in the trade and services sector grew by an average annual rate of 22.9 percent from 2000 to 2009, and this sector constituted 60.1 percent of total registered enterprises at the end of the period.[6] Currently, Vietnam's largest service industries are tourism, wholesale and retail services, repair of vehicles and personal goods, hotel and restaurants, transport and storage, and telecommunications.[7] By number of enterprises, the fastest-growing services industries between 2000 and 2009 were electricity, gas, and water; post and telecommunications; computers and related activities; and services supporting financial and monetary activities.[8]

Factors Affecting the Supply of Services in Vietnam

A number of factors affect the supply of services in Vietnam, with some fostering and others inhibiting the growth of service providers.

Support for Small and Medium-sized Enterprises (SMEs)

In an effort to encourage the growth of SMEs, the government of Vietnam has sought assistance from international donors such as the Asian Development Bank (ADB). Through an assistance program launched in 2004, the ADB funded various policy reforms, including a nationwide credit-guarantee system to support commercial bank lending to SMEs, as well as initiatives reducing the time needed to register a business and giving technical help to entrepreneurs. The $80 million program was correlated with a 20 percent compound annual growth rate in new SME registrations, with trade and services SMEs showing the fastest growth.[9] In 2007, 96,095 of Vietnam's 151,780 registered SMEs were involved with services.[10]

Liberalization

In some cases, loosening restrictions on services industries can increase efficiency, accessibility, innovativeness, and predictability. As part of its accession to the WTO, Vietnam took steps towards liberalizing services trade and allowed foreign ownership in most service industries. In 2010, disbursed FDI totaled $11 billion, up 10 percent from 2009 levels,[11] and in 2011 an estimated 3,190 out of 12,776 FDI projects were in services industries.[12] Construction accounted for the largest share of these projects (with a total of 738), followed by information and communication (661 projects) and wholesale retail and repair (556 projects).[13] However, while many services industries have been liberalized in recent years, the Vietnamese government is still heavily involved in production and investment throughout the economy, particularly in finance and telecommunications where state-owned enterprises (SOEs) are predominant (see the "Banking Services" section). Additionally, in some industries the country maintains trade barriers that insulate domestic suppliers from foreign competition (see the "Retail Services" section).

Skill Shortages

Services supply in Vietnam is held back by relatively low worker skill levels (see the "Education Services" section). In 2009, Vietnam's labor force of 47 million earned an average monthly wage of $84, compared to average monthly wages in the Philippines, Thailand, and China of $127, $253, and $393, respectively.[14] While access to cheap labor can increase the competitiveness of certain services industries, low wages can also reflect low levels of productivity and a limited ability to supply skill-intensive services. Post-secondary education in Vietnam is seen as subpar, and a recent survey by the World Economic Forum cited an inadequately educated workforce as a significant barrier to doing business in Vietnam.[15] Private firms such as General Electric and Intel have had to compensate for skill shortages among Vietnamese college graduates by setting up their own training facilities.[16]

Weak Business Environment

Transparency International's 2011 Corruption Perception Index ranked Vietnam 112 out of 183 countries,[17] and the 2009 Global Integrity Report gave Vietnam a score of 44 out of 100.[18] The latter report noted that the legal system offered little defense against actions of the government, in part because judiciary independence is limited.[19] The Vietnamese government recognizes that corruption has stunted economic development and has sought international aid in curbing the problem.[20] Even in the absence of corruption, vague and ill-designed regulations obstruct the operations of Vietnamese businesses and deter foreign businesses from entering the country. In its 2012 *Doing Business* report, the World Bank ranked Vietnam 98 (out of 183) in terms of its business environment, down from 90 in 2011. While recent reforms have raised standards of accountability for company directors, the country still scored poorly on investor protections.[21]

Lack of Infrastructure

Vietnam's ports, roads, and railways are inefficient, and the linkages among transport modes act as bottlenecks. Vietnamese ports have limited capacity, and businesses as well as Vietnamese officials have cited the ports' inadequacy as an obstacle to business development and trade (see the "Logistics Services" section).[22]

Factors Affecting the Demand for Services in Vietnam

Demand for services in Vietnam has increased for a variety of reasons, driving growth in key service industries.

Rising Wages

While average Vietnamese wages are lower than in neighboring nations, they have steadily risen at a compound annual growth rate of 6 percent from 2000 to 2009,[23] providing Vietnamese workers with more disposable income. By one estimate, Vietnamese disposable income reached $84 million in 2011, up from $64 million in 2008.[24] Growing disposable income has boosted demand for consumer services such as education and telecommunications; for example, mobile phone subscriptions increased to 154 million users in 2010, up from 110 million users in 2009 (see the "Telecommunications Services" section).[25]

Business Development

Businesses rely on intermediary services such as logistics, banking, and telecommunications to conduct day-to-day operations. Private businesses have flourished in Vietnam: the number of registered non-state-owned enterprises increased from 35,004 in 2000 to 196,776 in 2007.[26] A 2009 survey of over 2,000 Vietnamese businesses found that 98 percent of them regularly used the Internet and 36 percent sold goods and services online, suggesting that further private sector growth will continue to drive demand for computer services.[27]

Urbanization

Migration to the cities has concentrated businesses and made them more accessible to Vietnamese consumers, increasing demand for the services that these firms provide. In 2010, 30 percent of the Vietnamese population lived in urban areas, and the urbanization rate is expected to grow by 3 percent annually between 2010 and 2015.[28] Furthermore, 70 percent of all registered businesses were located in urban areas, particularly Hanoi and Ho Chi Minh City, in 2009.[29]

Besides health and education, urbanization has directly spurred demand for municipal transportation, electricity, and sanitation services. The government recognizes the importance of an efficient urban transportation system, and Vietnam's modernization plan emphasizes the need to overhaul infrastructure over the next decade.[30]

Comparison to Other ASEAN Countries

While the performance of Vietnam's services sector lags behind that of most other ASEAN members, its growth prospects are promising. Among ASEAN countries,[31] the average percentage of GDP dedicated to services industries in 2010 was 45.1 percent. Services accounted for 71.7 percent of Singapore's GDP, 55.1 percent of Philippines's GDP, 43.0 percent of Thailand's GDP, and 38.3 percent of Vietnam's GDP.[32] Vietnam's expected 2012 service industry growth of 6.2 percent is on par with the expected growth of services in Thailand (6.6 percent)[33] and exceeds the Philippines' forecasted growth (2.0 percent),[34] but falls short of Indonesia's (8.2 percent).[35] Vietnam's labor productivity, while starting from a low base, is expected to grow by 3.8 percent between 2011 and 2020 as the private sector grows and adopts new technologies,[36] compared to 3.9 percent for Thailand,[37] 3.2 percent in Singapore,[38] and 3.0 percent in Philippines.[39] ASEAN countries are planning to establish an economic community by 2015 which will allow unrestricted flows of services and investment between member countries. This will help Vietnam's services industries to further liberalize and integrate into the international economy.

References

Asia Development Bank (ADB). "Viet Nam: Small and Medium-Sized Enterprise Development Program Cluster: Subprograms I and II," December 2009. http://www.adb.org/Documents/PCRs/VIE/38335-01-vie-pcr.pdf

CIA, *see* U.S. Central Intelligence Agency (CIA).

Economist Intelligence Unit (EIU). "Indonesia Economy, Politics and GDP Growth Summary." http://country.eiu.com/indonesia.

———. *Long-Term Outlook: Philippines*, 2011. http://country.eiu.com/article.aspx?articleid=1128197897.

———. *Long-Term Outlook: Singapore*, 2011. http://country.eiu.com/article.aspx?articleid=48192589.

———. *Long-Term Outlook: Thailand,* 2011. http://country.eiu.com/article.aspx?articleid=1408359525.

———. *Long-Term Outlook: Vietnam,* 2011. http://country.eiu.com/article.aspx?articleid=1018443486.

———. "Philippines Economy, Politics and GDP Growth Summary." http://country.eiu.com/philippines (accessed February 15, 2012).

———. "Thailand Economy, Politics and GDP Growth Summary." http://country.eiu.com/thailand (accessed February 15, 2012).

———. "Vietnam Economy, Politics and GDP Growth Summary." http://country.eiu.com/vietnam (accessed February 15, 2012).

Euromonitor International. "Country Factfile: Vietnam." http://www.euromonitor.com/vietnam/countryfactfile (accessed June 14, 2011).

Foreign Investment Agency of Vietnam. "Information about FDI." http://fia.mpi.gov.vn/News.aspx?ctl=newsdetail&p=2.46&aID=1093 (accessed June 22, 2011).

Global Integrity Report. "Vietnam: 2009." http://report.globalintegrity.org/Vietnam/2009 (accessed February 15, 2011).

Government of Vietnam. General Statistics Office (GSO). *The Enterprises in Viet Nam 9 Years at the Beginning of Century 21*. Hanoi: GSO, 2010. http://www.gso.gov.vn/defaulten.aspx?tabid=515&idmid=5&ItemID=9775

———. *Enterprises' Data of the Year 2000–2008: Principle Indicators of Enterprises by Type of Ownership and Activities* (sic), 2009. http://www.gso.gov.vn/defaulten.aspx?tabid=515&idmid=5&ItemID=9775 (accessed July 21, 2011).

Government of Vietnam. Prime Minister. "Decision No. 175/QD-TTg of January 27, 2011, Approving the Overall Strategy on the Development of Vietnam's Service Sector through 2020," January 27, 2011. http://vbqppl.moj.gov.vn/vbpq/en/Lists/Vn%20bn%20php%20lut/ViewDetail.aspx?ItemID=107 39.

International Telecommunication Union (ITU). "Vietnam Ends December with 170 Mln Telephony Subs." January 13, 2011. http://www.itu.int/ITU-D/ict/newslog/Vietnam+Ends+December+With+170+Mln+Telephony+Subs.aspx.

Mackey, Michael. "Vietnam Seeks Billions for Ports Overhaul." *Asia Times Online,* December 9, 2009. http://www.atimes.com/atimes/SoutheastAsia/KL09Ae01.html.

Transparency International. "Corruption Perception Index 2011," 2011. http://cpi.transparency.org/cpi2011/results/.

U.S. Census Bureau. "2010 American Community Survey," 2010. http://www.census.gov/acs/www/.

U.S. Central Intelligence Agency (CIA). "Economy Overview: Vietnam." *World Factbook.* https://www.cia.gov/library/publications/the-world-factbook/geos/vm.html (accessed January 19, 2011).

U.S. Department of State. *Background Notes: Vietnam*, November 30, 2010. http://www.state.gov/r/pa/ei/bgn/4130.htm.

VietnamNet. "E-Commerce Set to Boom in 2010: Trade Ministry," February 16, 2010. http://en.baomoi.com/Home/economy/english.vietnamnet. vn/ Ecommerce-set-to-boom-in-2010- trade-ministry/42965.epi

World Bank. "Doing Business 2012: Doing Business in a More Transparent World," 2011. http://www.doingbusiness.org/reports/global-reports/doing-business-2012.

———. "World Development Indicators (WDI) Online Database." http://databank.worldbank.org/ddp/home.do (accessed February 15, 2012).

World Economic Forum. "The Global Competitiveness Report 2011–2012," 2011. http://www.weforum.org/reports/global-competitiveness-report-2011-2012.

International Trade in Services

Although Vietnam accounts for a small share of global trade in services, its total services trade volume (imports plus exports) has tripled since 1999.[40] From 1999 to 2008, both imports and exports increased at double-digit average annual rates. While exports dropped substantially in 2009 in the wake of the global economic downturn, in 2010, Vietnam's services trade recovered and resumed its growth trajectory, with a 21 percent increase in imports and 30 percent growth in exports (figure 1).[41]

Nonetheless, Vietnam remains a net importer of services with a growing services trade deficit. Service exports have risen over the past decade, as Vietnam's competitive advantages—strategic location, low costs, political stability, and a large workforce—have benefited manufacturing and service firms alike.[42] However, while profitable opportunities to support manufacturing industries have driven growth in some service industries, the country still relies heavily on imports of trade-related services. This is especially true of transportation services, which accounted for two-thirds of Vietnam's service imports in 2010 (figure 2).[43]

In 2010, tourism was Vietnam's largest commercial service export, accounting for almost two-thirds of all such exports.[44] Vietnam hosted over 5 million foreign visitors in 2010, more than double its 1.8 million visitors in

1999; most were leisure tourists.[45] Vietnam is a desirable tourist destination due to its unique natural resources and historical sites, particularly the seven destinations granted status as UNESCO World Heritage sites.[46] Vietnam's tourism industry has also benefited from the economic development and growing discretionary incomes of its regional neighbors, particularly China.[47] The government has supported the industry[48] by prioritizing development of the aviation sector and by recently ratifying an aviation agreement with Australia which will increase the number of flights between the two countries.[49]

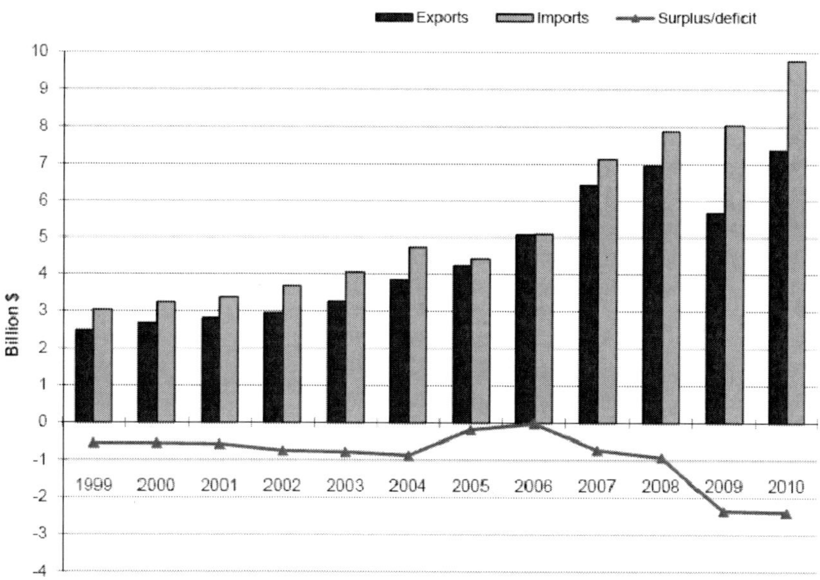

Source: WTO, International Trade Statistics 2011, 2011, 189–94, tables A8 and A9; International Trade Statistics 2010, 2010, 189–94, tables A8 and A9.

Figure 1. During 1999–2010, Vietnam's imports and exports of services more than doubled, and the country incurred a growing services trade deficit.

Outbound tourism from Vietnam has also increased in recent years, and travel services are Vietnam's second-largest services import. The majority of outbound tourists from Vietnam travel within the Southeast Asian region; however, a growing number of tourists travel to the United States and Europe.[50] Increasing English fluency, greater Internet access, growing comfort with independent travel, and the presence of budget airlines have given Vietnamese tourists greater control over their travel plans and reduced the need for travel agencies, particularly for destinations that do not require visas, such as the ASEAN member countries.[51]

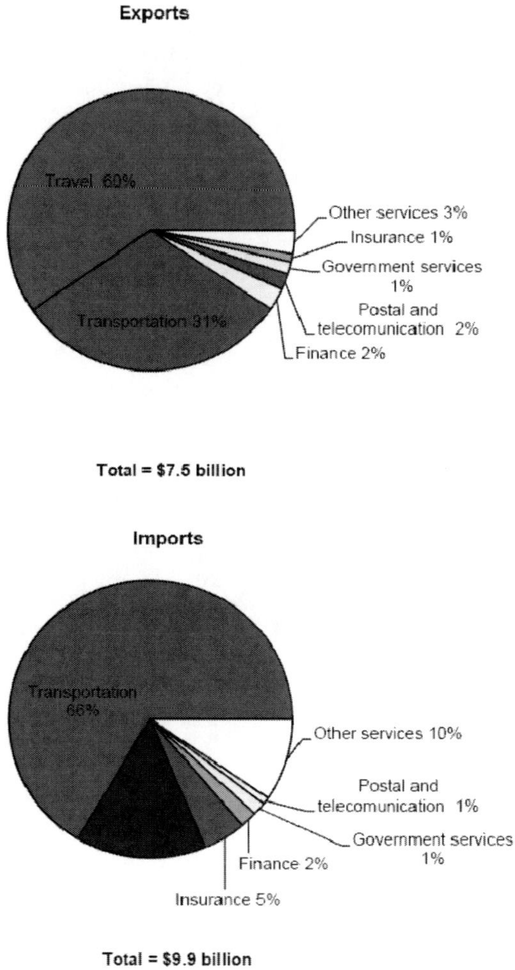

Source: Government of Vietnam, General Statistics Office, “Exports and Imports of Services, 2005–2010,” n.d. (accessed November 16, 2011).

Note: Totals are preliminary 2010 estimates by the General Statistics Office of Vietnam and may differ from thowe found in other sources.

Figure 2. Travel and transportation accounted for the bulk of Vietnam's exports and imports of services in 2010.

With the exception of tourism and travel, Vietnam trades few services other than those involved in the manufacture and movement of goods.[52] However, over the past decade, Vietnam's participation in a growing number of trade agreements has driven modernization and pro-market reforms that support the development of services sectors.[53] The U.S-Vietnam bilateral trade agreement (BTA) and Vietnam's WTO membership both required Vietnam to make legal reforms addressing foreign exchange regulations, SOEs, discriminatory price controls, and intellectual property, among other issues.[54] These reforms have facilitated trade in services by improving transparency and increasing regulatory certainty for domestic and foreign firms.[55]

Within Asia, the Republic of Korea (Korea) reports the largest volume of services trade with Vietnam.[56] Over the past five years trade in services between the two countries has grown rapidly: Korea imported $1.58 billion in services from Vietnam in 2009, more than double the $770 million in services Korea imported in 2005 and just under the $1.62 billion in services imported from Vietnam by all European Union (EU) countries in that year.[57] Services trade between the two countries is expected to continue to grow. Further, Korean firms already established in Vietnam will boost services trade by demanding more services for their operations.[58] Cultural and historical similarities are frequently cited as driving forces for the cooperation and strong trade relationship between Vietnam and Korea.[59] The two countries have launched a joint committee to study the benefits of formalizing their trade relationship through a bilateral free trade agreement (FTA).

Several factors have contributed to Vietnam's increasing role in regional services trade. Investors in Japan, Australia, and Hong Kong are attracted by Vietnam's low wages, geographic location, stable political regime, and growing domestic market, among other competitive advantages.[60] In particular, Vietnam's services trade has benefited from rising labor costs in China and a preference among regional manufacturers to diversify their production base beyond China.

Multinationals from Japan, Korea, Hong Kong, and Taiwan, as well as some from mainland China, have moved production to Vietnam, which has raised demand for supporting services such as transportation, warehousing, and trade-related financial services.[61] As a result, Vietnam is increasingly viewed as a gateway to both the ASEAN and Chinese markets.[62]

However, several factors inhibit Vietnam's service sector growth, many stemming from government policies. Among other challenges, SOEs continue to operate in a number of Vietnam's service sectors.[63]

The continued presence of SOEs impedes growth and competitiveness by introducing market distortions, as these enterprises frequently receive government investment and other forms of preferential treatment. SOEs are the leading recipients of Vietnamese government investment, and by one estimate state capital is roughly half as productive as private capital in Vietnam.[64] In 2007, the government announced its intentions to reduce the role of SOEs by privatizing most, excepting those in "strategic sectors."[65] However, SOEs continue to operate in key service industries—aviation, travel, telecommunication, banking, electricity, marine transportation, and insurance[66]—and in 2009 they accounted for roughly 38 percent of Vietnam's GDP.[67]

Service firms also face challenging and time-consuming regulations.[68] For example, Vietnam's tourism industry remains smaller than its regional competitors (figure 3) and attracts fewer return visitors[69] in part because of a lengthy and confusing visa application process.[70] A representative of the tourism lobby in Vietnam reported that the country was recently passed over for the filming of a major motion picture due to the perceived difficulty of obtaining visas, licensing, and approval to film, as well as the logistics of moving around the country.[71]

Although the industry has called for reforms to the visa process and the country wants to promote and support its largest exporting service industry, Vietnam's government also wants to maintain strict control over entry into the country—in part, reportedly, as a response to other countries' strict entry requirements for Vietnamese citizens.[72] Further, unlike the Malaysian government's award-winning "Malaysia: Truly Asia" marketing drive, Vietnam's government has yet to launch a successful international tourism campaign.[73] In 2010, Hanoi marked its 1,000-year anniversary as the nation's capital with a week-long celebration, but the national tourism authority did little to promote the event.[74]

Despite these challenges, Vietnam's government has made progress in its transition toward a market economy over the past 15 years, promoting growth in services and implementing reforms needed to establish normal economic relationships with all major powers for the first time.[75] The government recognizes the importance of competitiveness and global integration in its services industries, and continues to improve the business environment. For example, in 2010, the government simplified over 250 administrative procedures across multiple ministries.[76]

Vietnam continues to focus on international integration by participating in bilateral and multilateral trade organizations and agreements.

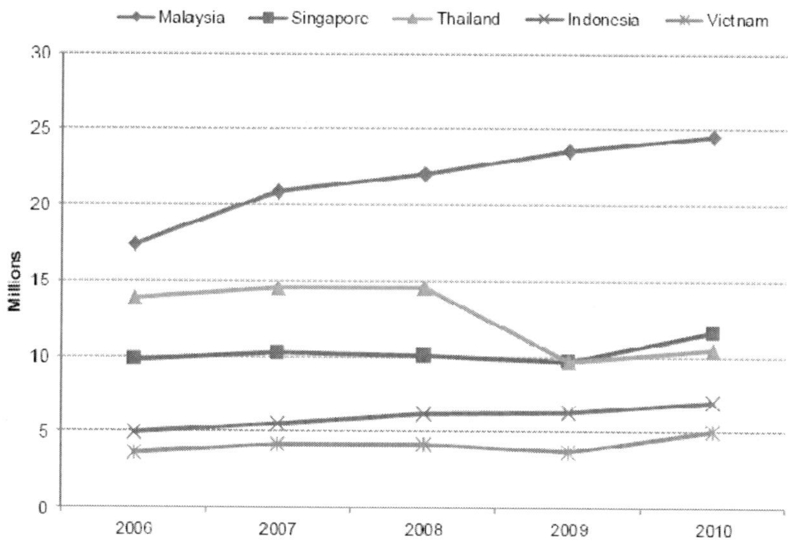

Sources: Singapore Tourism Board, *Annual Report on Tourism Statistics 2009*, October 2010; Singapore Tourism Board, "Fact Sheet," February 10, 2011; Tourism Malaysia, "Tourist Arrivals and Receipts to Malaysia," 1998–2010 (n.d.); Tourism Authority of Thailand, "Tourism Statistics in Thailand 1998–2007," May 6, 2008; Baden Pusad Statistic (Statistics Indonesia), "Number of Foreign Visitor Arrivals by Port of Entry 2008-September 2011," and "Number of Foreign Visitor Arrivals by Port of Entry 1997–2008;" GSO, "Number of Foreign Visitors to Vietnam, 1995–pre 2010," n.d . (accessed November 16, 2011).

Figure 3. Vietnam hosted fewer visitors than its neighbors during 2006–10.

Vietnam Has Rapidly Developed International Trade Relationships

Since the mid-1990s, Vietnam has sought to create a competitive, globally integrated economy by participating in a growing number of trade agreements. Initially focused on Asian markets, Vietnam has become more independent and sophisticated in pursuing relationships with countries further afield. This engagement has led to stronger diplomatic relations with a number of countries, including the United States (box 1).

Many of Vietnam's first formal trade relationships occurred via regional trade organizations, particularly ASEAN (which Vietnam joined in 1995) and the Asia-Pacific Economic Partnership (joined in 1998).[77] Vietnam's membership in ASEAN—particularly its participation in the 2006 ASEAN Free Trade Agreement—substantially deepened its regional economic relationships. In the past few years, ASEAN has entered into trade agreements with a number of significant markets, including Korea, India, Australia, New Zealand, and China.[78]

Box 1. U.S.-Vietnam Relations in the Shadow of China

China's rise and increasing dominance in Asia has been a defining factor in U.S.-Vietnam relations. After more than 15 years of having no economic or diplomatic ties, the United States normalized relations with Vietnam in 1995 and signed a bilateral trade agreement in 2000.[a] Since then, economic links between the two countries have grown progressively stronger.

This deepening strategic relationship has allowed both countries to achieve leverage with China.[b] The 2007 Trade and Investment Framework Agreement with Vietnam offers U.S. firms a regional alternative to China, diversifying the U.S. presence in Asia and reducing reliance on China for manufacturing and production.[c] It also limits the extent to which U.S. firms operating abroad could face negative consequences as a result of U.S. pressure on China concerning trade issues and currency reform.[d] In turn, Vietnam's strengthened relationship with the United States has reduced its economic vulnerability resulting from an entrenched trade deficit with China. China is Vietnam's largest trading partner and the source of most of its imports; in 2010 China accounted for $11.6 billion of Vietnam's total trade deficit of $12.4 billion.[e] (Vietnam largely imports high-value finished goods and technology from China, while primarily exporting raw materials; many industries in Vietnam do not have the scale or efficiency to compete with China on price, so Vietnam's exports have not achieved significant market penetration there.) Vietnam's relationship with the United States has also provided leverage in military and political discussions with China. In 2010, with U.S. support, Vietnam forced China to address ongoing territorial disputes in the South China Sea (where conflicting territorial claims have persisted for decades) in open multilateral negotiations for the first time.[f]

Despite mutual economic and strategic benefits, important issues continue to complicate the U.S.-Vietnam relationship, illustrating the challenge Vietnam faces in striking a balance between socialism and capitalism, and between regionalism and internationalism.

Although Vietnam has embraced a market-based economic policy, its one-party political system continues to suppress political and religious dissent and censor social networking sites. This has ignited concerns in the United States regarding human rights, resulting in public reprimands that are a source of tension in the bilateral relationship.

For example, during a 2010 event commemorating 15 years of normal trade relations between the United States and Vietnam, U.S. Secretary of State Hillary Clinton called on Vietnam to reform and improve its human rights record.[g] Further, the Vietnamese government continues to seek deeper relations with China, a goal that is necessary given Vietnam's economic and geographic realities, but one that is complicated by and possibly contradictory to strengthening its relationship with the United States.[h]

[a] Manyin, "U.S.-Vietnam Relations in 2010," August 6, 2010, 10.

[b] EIU, "Vietnam," September 2011, 5.

[c] VentureOutsource.com, "U.S., Vietnam: Trade Ties and a China Buffer," June 22, 2007.

[d] Ibid.

[e] Ha and Do, "Vietnam-China Trade, FDI, and ODA Relations," 2009, 375–76; Bland, "Chinese 'iPhones' for Sale," September 15, 2011; Le, "Vietnam's State Capitalism and the Rise of Southeast Asia," February 16, 2011.

[f] In addition to China and Vietnam, Brunei, Indonesia, Malaysia, and the Philippines all claim ownership over some portion of the disputed area, which includes oceans and islands and has strategic and economic importance due to nearby shipping lanes and energy deposits. The very existence of the talks marked a success for Vietnam, as China asserted that its claim to the territory gave it authority to resolve all disputes in private bilateral negotiations. Landler, "Offering to Aid Talks," July 23, 2010; Manyin, "U.S.-Vietnam Relations in 2011," July 26, 2011, 8.

[g] Landler, "In Visit, Clinton Criticizes Vietnam on Rights," July 22, 2010; EIU, "Vietnam," September 2011, 5.

[h] EIU, "Vietnam," September 2011, 5; Le, "Vietnam's State Capitalism and the Rise of Southeast Asia," February 16, 2011; Manyin, "U.S.-Vietnam Relations in 2010," August 6, 2010, 8.

Vietnam has also strengthened trade relationships with the United States and Europe. The 2001 U.S.-Vietnam BTA normalized economic relations with the United States and speeded Vietnam's WTO accession by committing Vietnam to the legal, regulatory, and administrative reforms necessary to meet WTO standards.[79] Although neither the United States nor Vietnam report data on bilateral trade in services, it is likely that services trade between the two countries grew as the United States rose from one of Vietnam's smallest to its largest export market for goods following the BTA.[80] The increased regulatory transparency and strengthened legal system associated with this agreement also led to growth in services trade with the EU: EU service exports to Vietnam more than doubled from 2006 to 2009.[81]

Vietnam's accession to the WTO in 2007 was the culmination of its efforts to enter the global market. Following its accession, Vietnam signed a Trade and Investment Framework Agreement with the United States in 2007 and completed negotiations for an FTA with Chile.[82] It also joined the Trans-Pacific Partnership, a group of 10 countries currently negotiating an Asia-Pacific trade agreement,[83] and plans to start FTA negotiations with the EU.[84] Compared to past trade agreements which largely happened under the umbrella of ASEAN, Vietnam has had an increasingly global focus in its trade engagement.

References

Badan Pusat Statistic (Statistics Indonesia). "Number of Foreign Visitor Arrivals by Port of Entry 2008– September 2011." http://dds.bps.go.id/eng (accessed August 3, 2011).

———. "Number of Foreign Visitor Arrivals to Indonesia by Port of Entry 1997–2008." http://dds.bps.go.id/eng (accessed August 3, 2011).

Bland, Ben. "Vietnam: Chinese 'iPhones' For Sale." *beyondbrics* (blog). FT.com, September 15, 2011. http://blogs.ft.com/beyond-brics/ 2011/ 09/15/vietnam-chinese-iphones-for-sale.

———. "Vietnam Tourism: Better Marketing?" *beyondbrics* (blog). FT.com, June 6, 2011. http://blogs.ft.com/beyond-brics/2011/0606/vietnam-tourism-better-marketing.

Cany, Alain. "Vietnam Business Forum: December 2, 2010." Eurocham Position Paper. European Chamber of Commerce in Vietnam, December 2, 2010.

Economist. "Laying a Thousand-year Egg," October 8, 2010.

Economist Intelligence Unit (EIU). "Vietnam." *Country Commerce Report*, April 2011.

———. "Vietnam." *Country Report*, September 2011.

European Chamber of Commerce in Vietnam (Eurocham). Tourism and Hospitality Sector Committee. "Position Paper—Tourism and Hospitality, 2011," 2011.

Freshfields Bruckhaus Deringer. "Vietnam—New Investment Law," March 2006. http://www.mekongresearch.com/doc/New%20Investment%20Law%20Sector%20Update.pdf.

Government of Australia. Department of Foreign Affairs and Trade. "Vietnam Country Brief," March 2011. http://www.dfat.gov.au/geo/vietnam/vietnam brief.html.

Government of Vietnam. "Resolution on Simplifying 258 Administrative Procedures under the Management Authorities of Ministries, Agencies." No. 25/NQ-CP, Hanoi, June 2, 2006.

———. General Statistics Office (GSO). "Exports and Imports of Services, 2005–pre-2010," n.d. (accessed November 16, 2011).

———. "Number of Foreign Visitors to Vietnam, 1996–pre-2010," n.d. (accessed November 16, 2011).

Government of Vietnam. Ministry of Foreign Affairs. "General Information about Countries and Regions," April 26, 2011. http://www.mofa.gov.vn/en/cn vakv/.

Government of Vietnam. Vietnam National Administration of Tourism Statistics (VNAT). "International Visitors to Vietnam in December and 12 Months of 2008." December 30, 2008.

———. "International Visitors to Vietnam in December and 12 months of 2009." January 10, 2010.

———. "International Visitors to Vietnam in June and 6 Months of 2011." June 30, 2011.

———. "International Visitors to Vietnam in December and 12 Months of 2010." January 6, 2011.

———. "Vietnam Okays Pact on More Flights to Australia." July 5, 2011.

Ha, Thi Hong Van, and Do, Tien Sam. "Vietnam-China Trade, FDI and ODA Relations (1998–2008) and the Impacts upon Vietnam." *BRC Research Report, no. 1*, 2009.

Saich, Anthony, Dwight Perkins, David Dapice, Vu Thanh Tu Anh, Nguyen Xuan Thanh, and Huynh The Du. "Choosing Success: The Lessons of East and Southeast Asia and Vietnam's Future." Harvard Vietnam Program, January 2008.

Hoekman, Bernard, and Aaditya Mattoo. "Services Trade and Growth." World Bank Policy Research Working Paper no. 4461, January 2008.

Hui, Tai, Thomas Harr, Edward Lee Wee Kok, and Danny Suwanapruti. "Vietnam—Rediscovering the Frontier." Standard Chartered Bank, May 31, 2010.

Indochine Counsel. "Client Alert," February 2011.

Kien, Tran Nhuan, Hong Ryul Lee, and Yoon Heo. "Dynamic Patterns of Korea–Vietnam Trade Relations." *International Area Review* 13, no. 2 (Summer 2010): 257–79.

Landler, Mark. "In Visit, Clinton Criticizes Vietnam on Rights." *New York Times*, July 22, 2010.

———. "Offering to Aid Talks, U.S. Challenges China on Disputed Islands." *New York Times*, July 23, 2010.

Le, Long S. "Vietnam's State Capitalism and the Rise of Southeast Asia." *Global Vietnamese Diaspora* (blog), Bauer College of Business, University of Houston, February 16, 2011. http://blogs.bauer.uh.edu/vietDiaspora/blog/vietnam%e2%80%99s-state-capitalism-and-the-riseof-southeast-asia/.

Lee, Il Houhg, Patrizia Tumbarello, Noel Sacasa, and Pritha Mitra. "Vietnam: Selected Issues." IMF Country Report No. 07/385, December 2007.

Lobet, Jean Michel. "Protecting Minority Shareholders to Boost Investment." *Doing Business: Celebrating Reform 2008*. Washington, DC: World Bank, 2008.

Manyin, Mark E. *U.S.-Vietnam Relations in 2010: Current Issues and Implications for U.S. Policy*. CRS Report for Congress 7-5700. Congressional Research Service, August 6, 2010.

———. *U.S.–Vietnam Relations in 2011: Current Issues and Implications for U.S. Policy*. CRS Report for Congress 7-5700. Congressional Research Service, July 26, 2011.

Nhi, Lan. "Service Sector's Sloping Playing Field." *Saigon Times*, November 5, 2010.

Organisation for Economic Co-operation and Development (OECD). OECD.Stat database. http://stats.oecd.org/index.aspx?r=668368 (accessed November 7, 2011).

Patrikainen, Maria. "Vietnam, Chile Conclude Successful FTA Negotiations." *Global Insight*, June 23, 2011.

Singapore Tourism Board. *Annual Report on Tourism Statistics 2009*, October 2010.

———. "Fact Sheet: Tourism Performance for Jan–Dec 2010," February 10, 2011.

TBKTVN [Vietnam Economic Times]. "Complicated Procedures Hinder Vietnam's Tourism Development." Vietnamnet.en, January 6, 2011. http://english.vietnamnet.vn/en/travel/8969/complicated-procedures-hinder-vietnam-s-tourismdevelopment.html (accessed August 3, 2011).

Tourism Authority of Thailand. "Tourism Statistics in Thailand, 1998–2007," May 6, 2008. Tourism Malaysia. "Tourist Arrivals and Receipts to Malaysia, 1998–2010" (n.d.).

Tran, Ngoc. "Vietnam and Korea Trade and Investment Ties Will Grow Strongly." *Saigon Times Online*, September 9, 2010.

U.S. Department of State. Bureau of Economic, Energy, and Business Affairs. "2011 Investment Climate Statement," March 2011.

VentureOutsource.com. "U.S., Vietnam: Trade Ties and a China Buffer," June 22, 2007.

Vietnam Ministry of Planning and Investment, Central Institute of Economic Management and Foreign Investment Agency and USAID-funded Support for Trade Acceleration Project. "Assessment of the Five-Year Impact of the U.S.-Vietnam Bilateral Trade Agreement." July 2007.

VNEconomynews.com. "Outbound Tourists Double in Number This Year." December 23, 2010. World Trade Organization (WTO). *International Trade Statistics 2010*, 2010.

———. *International Trade Statistics 2011*. 2011.

World Travel and Tourism Council. Economic Data Search Tool. http://www.wttc.org/research/economic-data-search-tool (accessed July 13, 2011).

BANKING SERVICES

Since the early 1990s, Vietnam's banking sector has evolved from a largely closed state-run industry to a more modern market-oriented system, and the number of private and foreign participants continues to grow steadily. The banking and financial sector has grown at twice the rate of Vietnam's GDP in recent years,[85] and the number of bank accounts has increased rapidly, though most Vietnamese still lack bank accounts. Despite this growth, the continued domination of the sector by state-owned commercial banks (SOCBs), which provide a large amount of (often nonperforming) loans to SOEs, poses a challenge to banking sector development. The increasing prosperity of the middle class will likely drive demand for more sophisticated banking services in the near future.

Vietnam's Banking Sector is Growing Quickly

Commercial banks are a vital source of credit for individuals and businesses in Vietnam.[86] Assets in the Vietnamese banking sector grew from $52.4 billion in 2007 to $128.7 billion in 2010, and were projected to reach $175.4 billion by the end of 2012.[87] Overall, the banking sector is projected to grow by 15 percent per year through 2015.[88] The total amount of domestic credit provided by the Vietnamese banking sector in 2010 was equal to 136 percent of the country's GDP, up from 35 percent in 2000. While this figure is still far less than the 204.1 percent of GDP in domestic credit provided by the banking sectors of all Organization for Economic Co-operation and Development (OECD) countries in 2010, it was about twice the average figure for ASEAN countries that year (figure 4).[89] Most of this growth has come from institutional banking; Vietnamese firms have demanded more sophisticated financial services as they have grown. The greater availability of such services has led an increasing number of foreign firms to establish operations in Vietnam.

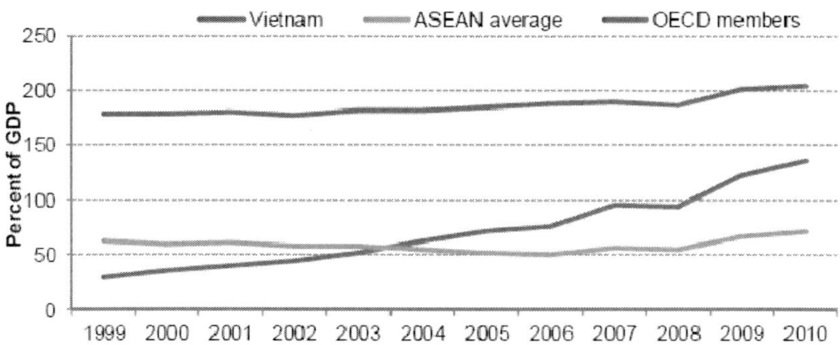

Source: World Bank, World Development Indicators database.

Figure 4. Domestic credit in Vietnam has tripled since 2002.

Vietnam's retail banking market is in its infancy. While the number of automatic teller machines per thousand adults increased from 3 in 2005 to 18 in 2010,[90] the use of consumer banking services remains limited, as only 20 percent of the Vietnamese population held bank accounts at the end of 2009.[91] Further, foreign consumers accounted for an estimated 89 percent of all Visa card sales transactions in Vietnam in 2006, suggesting low consumption of credit card services among nationals.[92] Most Vietnamese households rely on cash and trust-based informal credit networks, which comprise loans between relatives and friends as well as rotating savings associations and shopkeepers who sell agricultural inputs like seeds and pesticides on credit.[93] (A 1998 survey of Vietnamese households estimated that informal credit accounted for 51.2 percent of total domestic credit, though that share has likely decreased since.[94]) Distrust of banks among older consumers may stem from Vietnam's hyperinflation in the 1980s and currency depreciation in the 1990s, which encouraged people to use cash for transactions and store their wealth in commodities or foreign currencies. Additionally, potential borrowers often encounter challenges in Vietnam's formal banking sector; many lending institutions have stringent collateral rules (often requiring land titles, houses, or other fixed assets) and time-consuming loan application processes.[95]

As household incomes continue to rise, though, more Vietnamese will likely take advantage of savings vehicles such as pension plans and borrowing opportunities such as home mortgage loans, which will present growth opportunities for both Vietnamese and foreign banks. Rising demand for cars may be a particularly strong stimulant of loan activity in Vietnam.[96] Generational differences in demand for banking services also drive growth forecasts; one survey found that Vietnamese consumers aged 21–29 were more likely to own savings accounts and debit cards, and more willing to use Internet-based banking, than older consumers.[97]

The expansion of loans may facilitate growth in Vietnam's broader economy. Bank loans for short-term working capital and long-term fixed capital are a vital resource for entrepreneurs, especially in countries where investors and venture capitalists are scarce. As of 2010, only an estimated 30 percent of SMEs in Vietnam had had credit transactions with banks.[98] Such transactions are partly limited by the policies of Vietnamese banks; for example, SOCBs provide unsecured lending only to private enterprises with at least two consecutive years of profits, a rule that excludes start-up businesses.[99] This suggests there may be unmet demand for credit.

However, Vietnam's rapid expansion of credit has already resulted in rising amounts of bad loans. Nonperforming loans held by Vietnamese banks reportedly equaled 3.2 percent of total outstanding loans in 2011, though the actual number may be higher given pressure on banks to roll over or recategorize such loans.[100] Business loans to SOEs are a notable contributor; Vietnamese SOEs are often unprofitable (partly because many use outdated management strategies designed for a centrally planned economy), but lenders often believe that loans to SOEs are implicitly guaranteed by the government, which reduces the incentive to evaluate borrowers rigorously. For instance,

Vinashin, a Vietnamese shipbuilding SOE that incurred losses due to unproductive investments, started missing loan payments in late 2010. As a result, ratings agencies (which had erroneously expected the government to support Vinashin) downgraded Vietnam's sovereign credit rating as well as the credit ratings of several Vietnamese banks, arguing that the Vinashin case highlighted the fact that "credit risk management and supporting infrastructure in Vietnam have not kept pace with rapid credit growth in the Vietnam banking system."[101]

According to one study, loans for business or consumption in Vietnam are riskier than housing loans, while loans to urban households are riskier than loans to rural households.[102]

Bank loans in foreign currencies are particularly risky, as they are exposed to exchange rate fluctuations; by one estimate, such loans accounted for over 20 percent of Vietnam's total loans in 2011.[103] These risks are exacerbated by weakness and unpredictability in formal institutions and legal frameworks, which limit lenders' recourse for recovering nonperforming loans. Too-rapid expansion of credit and high business failure rates join high inflation and liquidity shortages as the most serious (and interrelated) challenges to Vietnam's banking sector.[104]

One of the cross-cutting issues that weakens the banking sector and inhibits credit transactions in Vietnam is a lack of information. The credit histories of Vietnamese consumers and businesses are short, and as a result many loans are reportedly motivated by personal relationships instead of financial analysis.[105]

More generally, while banks seek out information about firms and the overall commercial environment when assessing the viability of business plans, the sources of such data (such as company registries kept at local Departments of Company Registration) are reportedly not kept up to date, partly due to the rapid growth of new businesses.[106] Banks often struggle to estimate the value of collateral such as houses.[107]

Additionally, weak corporate governance norms and a shortage of financial skills can result in inaccuracies or falsifications in the formal financial documents provided by firms seeking loans.[108] (Banks have incentives to determine the "real" financial situation of such firms, but the formal financial data provided on forms often have a stronger legal status.) Some banks respond to these challenges by using inefficient and elaborate monitoring processes. One bank allows a borrowing firm to hold one key to its inventory warehouse while the bank keeps a second key: both keys are required to access inventory.[109]

Industry Reforms Have Increased Competition

Until the late 1980s, the State Bank of Vietnam (SBV) was the only entity in the banking sector, acting as both central bank and primary commercial bank. Major reforms enacted through the 1990 Ordinance on the State Bank of Vietnam shaped a transition from this one-tier banking system to a more competitive market-based system. The SBV became the country's central bank, responsible for monetary policy and regulation, and relinquished all commercial banking functions to four newly established SOCBs—government-controlled banks initially designed to serve the needs of SOEs in various segments of the economy.[110] Currently the SBV controls reserve requirements, the foreign exchange trading band, and discount, refinancing, and base lending rates.

Vietnam enacted several additional banking reforms in the 1990s and early 2000s. Joint-stock commercial banks (JSCBs), which have both public and private shareholders, were established to operate more flexibly (i.e., without the social goals of SOCBs) and to serve SMEs. The government began partially privatizing SOCBs in 2006, intending to reduce government ownership to 51 percent, but this privatization process remains incomplete partly due to a lack of investors. (The fact that the SBV both supervises SOCBs and partially owns them raises concerns about conflicts of interest and preferential treatment.[111]) The reforms that established JSCBs also enabled foreign banks to enter Vietnam and bring capital and experience into the country. Foreign banks can enter the market through JSCBs, as branches, or as representative offices providing limited services.[112] In 2004, the government amended its banking laws to comply with its commitments under the U.S.-Vietnam BTA, which required Vietnam to allow 100 percent U.S.-owned subsidiary banks by 2010.[113] In doing so, the country effectively opened up the market to wholly owned subsidiary banks from any country, per Vietnam's obligations under its WTO accession agreement. Further, in January 2011 the Vietnamese government granted foreign bank branches national treatment, allowing foreign banks to provide the same range of services (and subjecting them to the same requirements) as domestic banks. However, Vietnam maintains a 49 percent equity cap on foreign bank holdings in joint ventures.

Vietnam's monetary authorities (like those in other countries) face tradeoffs in attempting to strengthen and reduce systemic risk in the banking sector. The SBV has steadily increased supervision and prudential regulation of Vietnamese banks, raising the minimum capital requirements for banks in 2010 to 3 trillion dong (or about $160 million), up from 2001 requirements of

5 billion dong ($340,000) for rural commercial banks and 50–70 billion dong ($3.4–4.8 million) for urban banks.[114] This promoted consolidation among smaller banks, which are more likely to fail (though larger banks cause more damage in the event of failure).

Vietnam also struggles with inflation, which peaked as high as 28 percent in 2008, and the SBV's tight monetary policy has raised the cost of loans. (Anti-inflation efforts increased the 2011 borrowing costs for one-year dong-denominated loans to 20 percent, compared to 12 percent in 2010.)[115] The SBV's efforts are occasionally undercut by a lack of clear guidance; for example, in May 2011, the SBV issued a statement on the eligibility criteria of investors in SOCBs, but did not explain whether foreign banks' owning a stake in other commercial banks would be a conflict of interest.[116]

Foreign Banks are Expanding Their Presence in Vietnam

SOCBs dominate the banking sector, holding 51 percent of total assets in 2008 (table 1). However, this figure represents a steady decline from 67 percent in 1997.[117] JSCBs, on the other hand, have steadily increased their market share over the past decade, mainly at the expense of SOCBs. Just in the three years from 2006 to 2008, JSCBs and foreign banks saw their share of assets grow by 42 and 5 percent respectively.[118] Foreign firms' share of assets in the Vietnamese banking sector has continued to grow since 2008 due to further liberalization.

As mentioned earlier, SOCBs tend to hold a large amount of nonperforming loans, a consequence of channeling credit to rural borrowers and SOEs. In 2010, SOCBs accounted for 49 percent of Vietnam's total lending but held an estimated 60 percent of the country's nonperforming loans.[119] In 2006 and 2007, the average rate of return on assets for most of the major SOCBs were below the average for Asian banks, and their capital adequacy ratios were below Asia-Pacific regional averages.[120]

Foreign banks are eager to expand operations in Vietnam, as they anticipate rapid growth in demand for banking services. Most foreign banks enter the Vietnamese market as JCSBs or branches; as of 2008 only five foreign firms had been granted licenses to operate as wholly owned foreign banks in Vietnam.[121] In late 2011, the SBV allowed both the Commonwealth Bank of Australia and Singapore's United Overseas Banks to increase their holdings in Vietnam International Commercial Joint-Stock Bank and Southern Commercial Joint-Stock Bank, respectively, to 20 percent.

Table 1. Number of banks in Vietnam by type and assets, 2008

Type of bank	Number of institutions	Share of assets (%)
State-owned commercial banks	5	51.48
Joint stock commercial banks	40	32.45
Foreign bank branches	45	10.26
Wholly foreign-owned banks	5	([a])
Joint venture banks	5	1.25

Source: EU-Vietnam MUTRAP, "Comprehensive Strategy for Service Sector Development," December 2009, 292.

Notes: [a]Five wholly foreign-owned banks had been approved by 2008 but had not yet become operational at that time.

Additionally, in 2011 Mizuho Financial Group of Japan bought a 15 percent stake in Vietcombank for $567 million, the largest purchase of its kind in Vietnamese history.[122] However, Vietnam continues to limit the growth of foreign banks by capping debt growth at 20 percent and requiring foreign bank debt to be on the balance sheet of the local firm, not the parent firm.[123]

Foreign banks have largely been successful in Vietnam, due in part to demand from multinational firms, particularly those needing trade finance and foreign exchange services. Local banks have some advantages over foreign banks in their ability to access inexpensive inputs, as foreign banks tend to spend more on professional branding and marketing activities (for example, in 2008 local JSCB Lien Viet Bank spent only $10,000 on developing the bank's logo design and $5,000 on the bank's slogan).[124] However, foreign banks are viewed as providing higher quality retail banking services than their Vietnamese counterparts, and their presence in the market creates additional pressure to modernize the domestic banking industry.[125] By some accounts, Vietnamese banks are less transparent and more likely to use risky management practices than foreign banks are, so greater involvement from foreign banks may make Vietnam's banking sector more resilient.[126] As rapid growth and inflationary pressures increase demand for capital, Vietnam is likely to seek more involvement from foreign banks.

References

Andrade, Nigel P., Jens Lottner, and Christian Roland. "How Young Consumers Could Shape Vietnam's Banks." *McKinsey Quarterly,* March

2008. http://www.vinacapital.com/userfiles/file/how young consumers vietnam banks.pdf.

Business Advantage Vietnam. "Reforms Open Up Banking Sector," 2010. http://businessadvantagevietnam.files.wordpress.com/2010/02/businessad vantagevietnam2010_p 14 15.pdf.

Chan, Jason. "New State Bank of Vietnam Guidelines Lack Clarity for Foreign Shareholders." *International Financial Law Review* 30, no. 5 (June 2011).

EU-Vietnam MUTRAP. "Comprehensive Strategy for Service Sector Development to the Year 2020 with a Vision up to 2025," December 2009.

International Monetary Fund (IMF). International Financial Statistics database. http://elibrarydata.imf.org/ (accessed February 28, 2012).

Federal Reserve Bank of San Francisco. "Asia Focus: Banking Reform in Vietnam," June 2011. http://www.frbsf.org/publications/banking/ asia focus/2011/june-banking-reform-in-vietnam.pdf.

Fitch Ratings. "2011 Outlook: Asia-Pacific Banks." January 31, 2011. http://www.asianbondsonline.adb.org/publications/external/2011/Outlook Asia Pacific Banks 2 011.pdf.

Kovsted, Jens, John Rand, and Finn Tarp. "From Monobank to Commercial Banking: Financial Sector Reforms in Vietnam." *Nias Reports*, June 30, 2006.

Leung, Suiwah. "Banking and Financial Sector Reforms in Vietnam." *ASEAN Economic Bulletin* 26, no. 1 (2009).

Maomi, Iwase. "Current Situation on Consumer Credit in Vietnam: Legal Framework for Formal Financial Sector." *Japan Social Innovation Journal* 1, no. 1 (2011). http://www.ips.uhyogo.ac.jp/jsij/wp-content/uploads/2011/04/40-45-Iwase Current-Situation-on-Consumer-Credit.pdf.

McNulty, Lucy. "In-house Wary over Banks' Vietnam Investment." *International Financial Law Review* 30, no. 8 (September 2011).

Nguyen, Thang, Ngoc Le, and Nick Freeman. "Trust and Uncertainty: A Study of Bank Lending to Private SMEs in Vietnam." *Asia Pacific Business Review* 12, no. 4 (2006): 547–67.

Pham, Thi Thu Tra, and Robert Lensink. "Lending Policies of Informal, Formal and Semiformal Lenders: Evidence from Vietnam." *Economics of Transition* 15, no. 2 (2007).

Reuters. "S&P: Vietnam Banks' SOE Loans May Harm Creditworthiness," December 12, 2010. http://www.reuters.com/article/2010/12/13/markets-ratings-vietnambanksidUSWNA671520101213.

———. "Vietnam Banks' Bad Debt Ratio Rises to 3.21 Pct in August," October 19, 2011.

http://www.reuters.com/article/2011/10/19/vietnam-bank-debt-idUSL3E7LJ07220111019.

Standard & Poor's. "Industry Report Card: Despite Varying Risks and Profitability, Southeast Asian Banks Are Likely to Remain Healthy," July 24, 2011. http://www.asifma.org/docs/sandp/IndustryReportCard Despite VaryingRisksandProfitabilitySoutheastAsianBanksAreLikelyToRemain Healthy.pdf.

Tran, Bao Toan. "Analysis of the Vietnamese Banking Sector with Special Reference to Corporate Governance." Doctoral dissertation, University of St. Gallen, 2008. http://www1.unisg.ch/www/edis.nsf/SysLkpBy Identifier /3412/$FILE/dis3412.pdf.

Vietnam Business News. "Banks Raise Chartered Capital by 600 Times in 9 Years," June 15, 2010. http://businesstimes.com.vn/banks-raise-chartered-capital-by-600-times-in-9-years/.

Waal, André, Hai Duong, and Vu Ton. "High Performance in Vietnam: The Case of the Vietnamese Banking Industry." *Journal of Transnational Management* 14, no. 3 (2009), 179–201.

World Bank. World Development Indicators and Global Development Finance database. http://databank.worldbank.org/ddp/home.do (accessed February 28, 2012).

EDUCATION SERVICES

Vietnam, a country in which two-thirds of the population is under the age of 30, is struggling to cope with a growing demand for higher education. The higher education sector in Vietnam has grown rapidly, adding 39 universities and 107 colleges since 2003[127] for a total of 150 universities and 226 colleges in 2009.[128] Nevertheless, there are places for less than 20 percent of Vietnam's one million annual high school graduates in Vietnamese institutions of higher education.

Partly for this reason, Vietnam has been actively seeking partnerships with foreign institutions, particularly those that offer high-demand programs like engineering and computer science.[129] Today, the main challenge facing

Vietnam's higher education and professional education industry is accommodating higher student enrollment while increasing educational quality and relevance.[130]

Economic Growth and Lack of High-Quality Institutions Drive Students Abroad

As the personal income of the population rises, more Vietnamese students are able to self-finance their higher education. However, with a shortage of quality colleges and universities at home, these students are looking outside of the country for better schooling options.

As of 2010, over 20,000 Vietnamese students were studying abroad, paying about $200 million annually in tuition and fees. Most study in the United States, United Kingdom, Australia, Canada, France, and Germany, as well as in other Asian countries that have strong higher education programs with a Western focus, such as Singapore and Hong Kong.

The United States has traditionally been the most desirable English-speaking destination for Vietnamese students, followed by Australia and the United Kingdom. However, Australia hosted more Vietnamese students than the United States in 2009, largely due to increased marketing campaigns funded by Australian universities and the country's national Chamber of Commerce.[131]

According to the Institute of International Education (IIE), 13,112 Vietnamese students studied in the United States during the 2009–10 academic year, ranking Vietnam ninth among countries sending students to the United States.[132] This reflects an increase of about 2 percent over the previous year's enrollment numbers, a small rise compared to increases of over 45 percent in each of the previous two academic years.

This difference can largely be attributed to the global economic downturn and to rapid inflation in Vietnam.[133] Overall, there has been a 380 percent increase in the number of Vietnamese students studying in the United States since the 1998–99 academic year. Vietnam ranks third among countries that send students to U.S. community colleges.[134]

Over half of these students study in California, Texas, and Washington. Most Vietnamese students that study in the United States eventually return to Vietnam to continue family businesses, join the civil service, or become lecturers or researchers at higher education institutions and research centers.[135]

Few Students Graduate from Vietnamese Institutions with Job-Ready Skills

The inadequate supply of skilled labor is an urgent matter in Vietnam, where skills development in universities has not matched employers' needs.[136] Vietnam has a high literacy rate (94 percent), largely due to near-universal primary education and a widely held respect for higher learning inherited from Confucianism.[137] However, the relatively small number of seats at Vietnamese universities and colleges limits access to technical training and higher education.

Further, graduates often lack practical expertise, as Vietnamese universities are generally mandated to produce a large number of graduates rather than achieve high educational quality or teach skills favorable to immediate employment.[138]

Current curriculum and course contents remain heavily oriented towards political theory (which accounts for up to 25 percent of the required coursework for undergraduates). Old Soviet approaches still exert great influence on the educational system as a whole; for example, there is little curricular emphasis on market economics.[139]

Teaching methods aimed at practical skills development, such as case studies, software training, and group discussions, are underused.[140] Many lecturers lack competency in high-demand subjects like computer skills and English communication.[141] Consequently, communication skills, while highly valued by employers, are reportedly given little attention in universities, and one survey found that Vietnamese graduates tend to lack teamwork skills.[142]

Weak university-industry linkages and the lack of public information on graduate employment and labor markets also impede the ability of Vietnam's education sector to meet the country's economic needs.[143] Surveys conducted by government-linked associations found that nearly 50 percent of Vietnamese university graduates were unable to find jobs in their area of specialization, illustrating a disconnect between classroom and market needs.

This gap was reflected in Intel's struggle to hire engineers to staff its manufacturing facility in Ho Chi Minh City several years ago: when the company administered a standardized assessment test to 2,000 Vietnamese IT students, only 90 candidates passed, and of this group only 40 had strong enough English skills to be hired. Intel indicated that this was the lowest pass rate they had encountered in any country where they invest.[144]

The Government is Heavily Involved in the Higher Education System

Strong government influence, particularly at the national level, limits the scope for improvements in the organization and administration of higher education institutions. Vietnam's Ministry of Education and Training (MOET) controls most aspects of the higher education system, including admissions policies, curriculum development, materials production, and student grading. Although MOET allows university and college administrators to suggest changes, there is no institutional recourse if their opinions are ignored. Compounding this is a lack of accountability for government officials and other public employees in higher education.[145] Additionally, government policies that affect private and nonprofit institutions create challenges. For example, nonpublic education and training institutions are subject to licensing provisions intended to guarantee minimum academic and public safety requirements. However, according to industry representatives, licensing procedures are slow, complicated, and inconsistent.[146] Nontraditional educational institutions such as film academies face particularly opaque licensing processes, as there is ambiguity about which laws apply and which licensing bodies have authority.[147]

As gross enrollment in higher education is expected to increase three- or fourfold by 2020, the Vietnamese government has introduced the Higher Education Reform Agenda (HERA) 2006–20 (box 2) to address these lingering bureaucratic inefficiencies.

Box 2. Vietnam's Higher Education Reform Agenda 2006–20

Since 1995, the Vietnamese government has actively sought to modernize its higher education system, which had remained largely unchanged since it was founded in the mid-1950s under Soviet influence. However, the government has been slow to make reforms due to a lack of resources and a time-consuming policymaking and regulatory environment. Vietnam's Higher Education Reform Agenda (HERA, or "Resolution 14") is a strategic plan enacted in 2005 that significantly increases the autonomy for Vietnamese universities and colleges in terms of personnel and financing.

HERA builds on previous reforms, including a 2002 decree (Decree 10/2002) that gave Vietnamese public institutions some autonomy to manage their own finances and seek alternative revenue sources.

As a result of these reforms, public higher education institutions in Vietnam can better diversify their revenue sources, collect more revenue, minimize spending on operations, lay off redundant employees, and increase wages for faculty and employees. HERA seeks to give education institutions more independence while promoting research-oriented academic planning and alignment with international standards. HERA also recognizes the need to increase the participation of the private and nonprofit sectors, anticipating that 40 percent of all higher education enrollments will shift into these sectors by 2020. To achieve this goal, Vietnam plans to further liberalize the entry requirements for private universities.

Sources: Vallely and Wilkinson, "Vietnamese Higher Education," November 2008, 3–6; Social Republic of Vietnam, Ministry of Education and Training, "Report," October 29, 2009, 19–23; Vietnam Business Forum, *Position Paper*, December 2007, 2–4; Asian Development Bank, "Viet Nam," August 2010, 16–21.

Vietnamese Universities and Colleges Are Not Internationally Competitive

In terms of quality, Vietnamese institutions of higher learning lag behind those of other Asian countries due to a relatively small professorate, weak faculty credentials, and poor infrastructure.[148] Faculty at Vietnamese universities and colleges numbered about 38,000 in 2006–07, while university students numbered about 1.2 million, resulting in a faculty-student ratio of 32 to 1.[149] With faculty salaries in Vietnam averaging about $150 per month (compared to $220–$250 for engineers and $500 for administrative officers),[150] there is little incentive for college graduates to go into teaching.[151] Moreover, the supply of faculty is constrained by the fact that only one-third of Vietnam's universities offer doctoral programs.[152] Hence, Vietnamese universities and colleges are increasingly using non-faculty or part-time lecturers to teach their classes.[153]

Vietnam's academics also have few publications and patents compared to other Asian countries. For example, in 2007, Seoul National University had 5,060 publications in peer-reviewed journals, while Vietnam National University (Hanoi and Ho Chi Minh City) and the Vietnam Academy of Science and Technology (Hanoi) published 52 and 44 papers, respectively. In

2006, Korean academics were awarded 102,633 patents, while Vietnamese researchers received none.[154] Further, in 2009 only about 14 percent of Vietnamese university faculty held doctoral degrees and only 33 percent had master's degrees,[155] with most degrees earned in Russia or other countries in the former Eastern Bloc. An August 2006 study conducted by the Vietnam Education Foundation of the National Academies of the United States found that Vietnamese lecturers had relatively weak research skills and academic knowledge, taught largely through lecturing and memorization, and had little interaction with students.[156]

Many universities still use equipment and facilities from the mid-1960s or 1970s. Libraries are often small and outdated, and are not electronically linked with a national library or central information system. Foreign literature is mainly in Russian and often dates from the mid-1970s. Even when universities have access to English-language literature, it is used infrequently due to the low level of English proficiency among faculty. These inadequate resources compound the shortcomings of teaching curricula that have been described as old, repetitive, and lacking in innovative approaches.[157]

Foreign Investment in Vietnam's Higher Education Sector Faces Challenges

Vietnam is seen as an attractive destination for foreign educational services firms looking for a foothold in the region. With the saturation of China's market and India's ban on foreign degree providers, a growing number of foreign institutions have sought partnerships with Vietnamese universities and colleges. Currently, hundreds of U.S. and other foreign institutions have signed memoranda of understanding with Vietnamese counterparts.

Dozens of these ventures offer dual-degree programs, and one pilot program allows local universities to hire American institutions to redesign their curricula and train their faculty members. Vietnam's MOET has actively encouraged these joint ventures.[158]

Nevertheless, many joint degree programs have quietly closed due to lack of returns or inertia.[159] According to one U.S. official, the signing of a cooperation agreement between a foreign education services firm and a Vietnamese institution is often followed by months of inaction by the Vietnamese partner, and around 80 percent of such international initiatives eventually fail. Reportedly, rivalries among Vietnamese universities are intense, and in some cases universities intentionally try to block the foreign partnerships of their competitors by limiting access to resources or sabotaging projects. In addition, some Vietnamese partner institutions oversell their programs to Vietnamese students and parents, which can damage the reputation of their foreign partners.[160]

However, some foreign colleges have succeeded in Vietnam. For example, Houston Community College (HCC) closely monitors its foreign campuses and holds frequent teaching workshops for its Vietnamese lecturers in order to maintain high academic standards.

Despite its annual tuition of $1,500 (almost 10 times what Vietnamese state universities charge), HCC's associate degree program grew from 400 to 3,000 students from 2003 to 2007.[161] Another example is Troy University, an Alabama-based institution which has a joint venture with Vietnam National University; it offers a master's program in business with a curriculum identical to that offered in the United States. The program costs about $4,800 a year—four times Vietnam's annual per capita income—but enrollment is consistently full.[162]

While Vietnam's openness to joint ventures has led to several high-quality degree programs, less scrupulous foreign ventures in Vietnam's education market are also becoming more common as lax rules governing partnerships with foreign universities allow unaccredited institutions to sell educational services easily.[163]

According to an official at IIE, the number of "rogue" or unaccredited distance-learning courses has steadily risen over the past several years, and little to no effort has been made by MOET to expel such providers from Vietnam.[164]

Vietnamese students who want to transfer to the United States or cite their degree in job applications sometimes find that their qualifications are worthless. For example, the State of Oregon's Office of Degree Authorization has declined to recognize degrees issued in Vietnam by Northcentral University, an online enterprise based in Arizona that offers an M.B.A. program in cooperation with the Hanoi University of Technology.[165] Moreover, in 2010, an inspection team under the direction of the Vietnamese National Assembly found that some universities were opening in Vietnam without a sufficient number of professors or a single physical location. Despite the growth of these unaccredited providers, at the time of writing the Vietnamese government has never used its authority to close a higher education institution.[166]

References

Asian Development Bank. "Viet Nam: Preparing the Higher Education Sector Development Project (HESDP)." Project No. 4207901, August 2010.

Ca, Tran Ngoc. "Universities as Drivers of the Urban Economies in Asia: The Case of Vietnam." World Bank Policy Research Working Paper 3949, June 2006.

Chronicle of Higher Education. "Private Universities in Vietnam Draw Fire from Government Investigators," April 13, 2010.

Di Gropello, Emanuela. "Vietnam: Higher Education and Skills for Growth." Paper presented at Regional Higher Education Conference: Strategic Choices for Higher Education Reform, Kuala Lumpur, Malaysia, December 3, 2007.

Economist Intelligence Unit (EIU). *Country Report: Vietnam*. London: Economist Intelligence Unit, June 2011.

Institute of International Education. "International Student Enrollments Rose Modestly in 2009/10, Led by Strong Increase in Students from China." Press release, November 15, 2010.

Int-Hout, Allison. "Vietnamese Students Overcome Hurdles to Study in America." *Northwest Vietnamese News,* February 16, 2011. http://www.nvnorthwest.com/vietnamese-students-overcome-hurdlesto-study-in-america/.

Library of Congress. "Education." In *A Country Study: Vietnam*. Federal Research Division, 1989. http://lcweb2.loc.gov/frd/cs/vntoc.html.

Organisation for Economic Co-operation and Development (OECD). *Education at a Glance, 2011: OECD Indicators*, 2011. www.oecd.org/dataoecd/61/2/48631582.pdf.

Overland, Martha Ann. "American Colleges Raise the Flag in Vietnam." *Chronicle of Higher Education*, May 15, 2009.

———. "As Vietnam Expands Its Higher-Education System, Professors Are in Short Supply." *Chronicle of Higher Education*, July 1, 2008.

Government of Vietnam. Ministry of Education and Training (MOET). "Report: On the Development of Higher Education System, the Solutions to Ensure Quality Assurance, and Improve Education Quality." No.760/BC-BGDDT. Hanoi, Vietnam: MOET, October 29, 2009.

Runckel, Christopher W. "The Education System in Vietnam." Business-in-Asia.com, 2009. http://www.businessin-asia.com/vietnam/education system in vietnam.html.

Saich, Anthony, Dwight Perkins, David Dapice, Vu Thanh Tu Anh, Nguyen Xuan Thanh, and Huynh The Du. "Choosing Success: The Lessons of East and Southeast Asia and Vietnam's Future." Harvard Kennedy School, Vietnam Program, January 2008.

Trung, Quang Trung, and Frederic William Swierczek. "Skills Development in Higher Education in Vietnam." *Asia Pacific Business* Review 15, no. 4 (October 2009): 565–86.

U.S. Department of Commerce (USDOC). U.S. Commercial Service. "Vietnam's Market for Education and Training," March 2010.

Vallely, Thomas J., and Ben Wilkinson. "Vietnamese Higher Education: Crisis and Response." Harvard Kennedy School. Ash Institute for Democratic Governance and Innovation, November 2008.

Vietnam Business Forum. *Position Paper on Developing Higher Education and Professional Education*, December 2007.

Vietnam Trade Office in the United States. "Business Environment," April 22, 2008. http://www.vietnam-ustrade.org/index.php?f=news&do=detail&id=35&lang=english.

Wasley, Paula. "Vietnamese Leaders, on U.S. Visit, Discuss Ambitious Overhaul of Higher Education." *Chronicle of Higher Education,* July 21, 2007.

LOGISTICS SERVICES

Logistics services comprise a range of activities that govern the end-to-end transport of raw, intermediate, and finished goods between producers and consumers. These services include freight forwarding, multimodal transport (i.e., transport by air, sea, road, and rail), and warehousing and storage. They also extend to value-added services such as customs brokerage, inventory management, order fulfillment, and product repair.[167]

Although some firms maintain in-house logistics capacity, most firms outsource all or part of their logistics requirements to third-party logistics providers (3PLs). The largest and most successful 3PLs offer an integrated package of logistics services, either by using their own transportation, information technology, and physical distribution assets, or by contracting out certain portions of the logistics supply chain (e.g., sea transport) to specialized firms.[168] 3PL activities are organized around extensive, and often global, transportation and supply chain networks, which provide operational and cost efficiencies to firms that, in turn, benefit their customers.[169]

Vietnam's Logistics Industry is Small but Growing

Vietnam's logistics industry, which consists of approximately 800 small-scale firms each providing a discrete set of services, is in an early stage of development.[170] There is little coordination among logistics service providers in Vietnam, so the industry is less efficient and more costly than in countries whose industries benefit from network and scale economies. Indeed, logistics costs in Vietnam account for an estimated 20 to 25 percent of the country's GDP[171]—a large proportion compared both to developed Asian countries such as Japan, South Korea, and Taiwan (9 percent each) and to nearby emerging markets such as China (18 percent), Malaysia (13 percent), and Thailand (16 percent) (table 2).[172]

Table 2. Comparison of logistics costs among selected Asian economies, 2009

Country	GDP ($ billion)	Logistics costs ($ billion)	Logistics costs (% GDP)
China	4,814	869	18.1
Hong Kong	211	19	9
India	1,095	142.8	13
Japan	5,108	444.4	8.7
Malaysia	193	[a]25	13
Singapore	165	14.9	9
South Korea	810	72.7	9
Taiwan	362	32.4	9
Thailand	264	42.2[(a)]	16
Vietnam	**93**	**18–23**	**20–25**

Source: Armstrong & Associates, Inc., "Global 3PL Market Size Estimates," 2011; Transport Intelligence, *Vietnam Logistics 2009*, February 2009, 45; *Bangkok Post*, "Transport Cost Cut Goal to Be Derailed," January 27, 2011.

Notes: [a]Estimated by Commission staff.

Nonetheless, revenue trends in Vietnam's logistics industry reflect its significant potential for growth. In 2005, the 3PL market in Vietnam was valued at $189 million;[173] by 2008, its value had more than doubled to reach $386 million, and it was expected to increase further to $528 million in 2012.[174] In 2009, 1.4 million workers were employed in Vietnam's transportation and storage industries (which include logistics), representing 3 percent of the country's total employment. By 2020, employment in these industries is projected to reach 1.5 million, an increase of 7 percent from 2009.[175] Vietnam's rapidly expanding role as a manufacturer of products for export—ranging from computer parts to textiles—is the primary impetus for the development of the country's logistics sector. The Vietnamese government has pledged to reduce logistics costs by increasing public and private investment in transportation infrastructure, including air and sea ports, roads, and railways.[176] Foreign investment in Vietnam's logistics industry is growing, particularly as large 3PLs from Asia, Europe, and the United States establish distribution and warehousing facilities near key economic and industrial zones in the country.[177] In addition, Vietnam has scheduled WTO commitments to fully liberalize foreign investment in the logistics industry in 2012, which will likely lead to further FDI increases.[178]

Vietnam Lacks Adequate Transportation Infrastructure

Vietnam's logistics industry is hobbled by the country's inadequate transportation infrastructure. At present, Vietnam has only seven deepwater ports and only four international airports, as well as a still-developing road and rail network (table 3).[179] The country's transport network is largely focused on three industrial zones: Hanoi in the north, Da Nang in central Vietnam, and Ho Chi Minh City in the south (figure 5).[180]

Table 3. Selected transportation infrastructure statistics for Vietnam

Number of seaports	49
Deepwater ports[(a)]	7
Largest port	Saigon Port cluster (Ho Chi Minh City)
Number of airports	44
International airports	4
Largest airport	Tan Son Naht (Ho Chi Minh City)
Roadways	171,392 kilometers (country comparison: 30[(b)])
Percent paved[(c)]	47
Railways	2,347 kilometers (country comparison: 67[(b)])

Sources: CIA, "Vietnam," March 8, 2011; General Statistics Office of Vietnam, "Some Main Indicators on Capacity of Transportation," 2008; Saigon Newport Holding Company, "Deep-water Ports and the Supporting Logistics Network," August 2009; Government of Vietnam, MPT, "Vietnam's IPs, EPZs and EZs," June 2007, 23; Transport Intelligence, *Vietnam Logistics 2009*, February 2009, 23.

Notes:

[a]Indicates ports with a capacity of 30,000 deadweight tons (dwts) or greater.

[b]Denotes rank among approximately 220 countries for which the CIA's *World Factbook* data are collected.

[c]Indicates percentage of roads that are paved with asphalt. In addition, about 4 percent of roads in Vietnam are paved with stone (or gravel); 22 percent are partially paved—that is, they consist of a mixture of dirt and gravel; and 27 percent are unpaved.

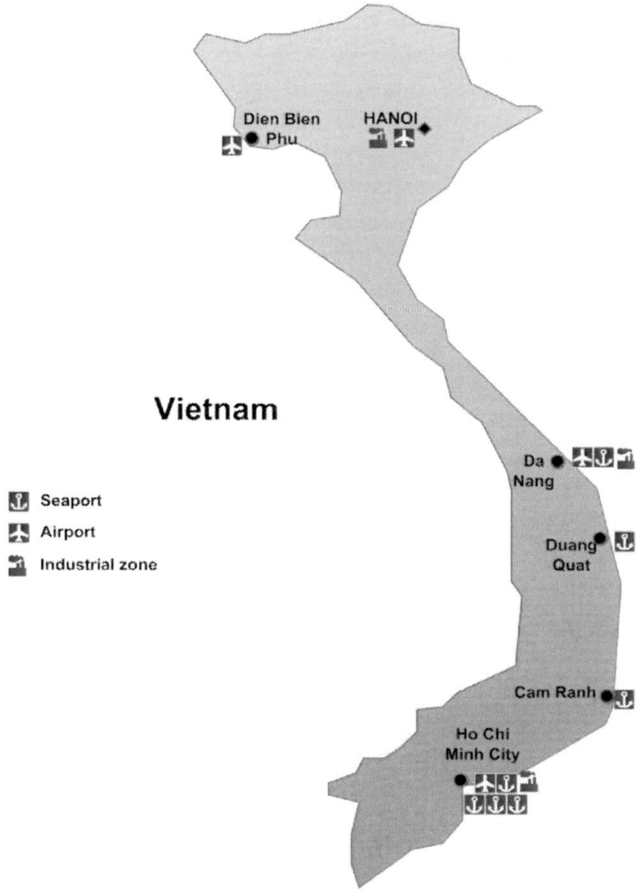

Source: Compiled by Commission staff.

Figure 5. Vietnam has a limited number of major air-and seaports, and most are clustered around industrial zones.

Sea transport is the primary mode of conveyance for Vietnamese exports and imports.[181] However, most of Vietnam's ports are not deep enough to accommodate large container ships; as a result, containerized cargo traveling between Vietnam and other countries is often transshipped via ports in Hong Kong, Singapore, and Taiwan, causing delays and increasing costs. In addition, even the largest and most sophisticated ports in Vietnam have too few container terminals, which leads to congestion.[182] Vietnam's underdeveloped port resources have kept the country from becoming a regional logistics hub, despite the increased activity of its manufacturing sector.[183]

Growing foreign investment, however, is helping to fill gaps in Vietnam's port infrastructure. Large international port operators DP World (United Arab Emirates) and Hutchison Port Holdings (Hong Kong) have partnered with the Vietnamese government to build and operate container terminals at Vietnam's largest port in Ho Chi Minh City.[184] Elsewhere, APM Terminals, a subsidiary of the Danish shipping firm A.P. Moller-Maersk, has constructed a container terminal outside of Hanoi in a joint venture with Vietnam's Vinashin Group.[185] APM Terminals has also invested in a series of container terminals near Ho Chi Minh City, scheduled to begin operating by 2013.[186]

Although air freight transport currently lags behind sea freight transport, the volume of air freight traffic in Vietnam is growing as more companies establish Vietnamese production facilities and Vietnam deepens transportation links with its neighbors.[187] Investment in Vietnamese airport infrastructure has increased in recent years, led principally by projects in the south. The largest project is the construction of Long Thanh International Airport near Ho Chi Minh City, slated to become Vietnam's largest international air hub in 2015, at which time 10 airports in Vietnam will serve international markets.[188] At present, Vietnam hosts more than 40 foreign airlines, including large logistics service providers such as DHL, FedEx, and UPS.[189] Improved airport infrastructure in Vietnam, together with further liberalization of the country's aviation market,[190] will likely increase the number of foreign airlines serving the Vietnamese market.

Finally, road and rail networks provide the critical link between airports, seaports, and markets for goods and services. Within the past 20 years, the Vietnamese government has invested heavily in roads, and to a more limited extent in railways.[191] However, many roads are still unpaved, and there are not enough highways to expedite the movement of passengers and freight.[192] In addition, Vietnam's rail network suffers from inadequate tracking and outdated rail equipment.[193] Currently, less than 2 percent of freight is transported by rail in Vietnam (compared to 70 percent by road), though this proportion is rising quickly.[194]

The government is planning major highway projects linking the northern city of Hanoi to Ho Chi Minh City in the south, as well as the northern town of Haiphong to nearby cities in China. In addition, in January 2011, the Vietnamese government began approving public-private partnerships (PPPs) to complete certain road and rail infrastructure projects, bringing in needed expertise and financial support.[195]

Customs Delays Hamper the Activities of Logistics Firms in Vietnam

The customs environment in Vietnam limits the supply of logistics services. Although the average customs clearance time for imports is four days—not unusual for a developing economy—rules and regulations are applied inconsistently, and customs inefficiencies are compounded by excessive paperwork, the lack of automated systems for customs processing, and fees.[196] In many developing countries, good customs administration practices are an important element in lowering the costs of trade. According to a recent World Bank Doing Business survey, Vietnam ranks 63rd among 183 countries in terms of its trading environment—below Singapore, Thailand, Malaysia, Indonesia, and the Philippines.[197] It takes an estimated 21 to 22 days to export and import goods from Vietnam, which makes it difficult for logistics firms to manage time-sensitive supply chains.[198]

Multinational Firms Drive Demand for Comprehensive Logistics Services

While local Vietnamese firms prefer to use small 3PLs for individual services such as freight transportation and customs clearance,[199] multinational firms, such as those in the high-tech, textiles, and apparel sectors, increasingly seek comprehensive, end-to-end logistics services.[200]

Many of these firms are located in one of Vietnam's nearly 150 industrial parks and export processing zones, which are designed to attract foreign manufacturing operations.[201] For example, in 2006, U.S.-based Intel invested $1 billion in a semiconductor assembly and testing plant in Saigon Hi-Tech Park near Ho Chi Minh City.[202] Other large firms, such as Japan-based Nidec and Singapore-based Jabil, are also located in the industrial park, increasing the need for supply chain service providers with expertise in the high tech and computer industries.[203]

Separately, the emergence of Vietnam as a leading exporter of fashion and apparel in Southeast Asia recently motivated Germany-based DHL to establish the first "fashion logistics" center serving the Vietnamese garment industry.[204] Logistics service providers, such as Switzerland-based Kuehne + Nagel, have also met the increasing demand for the movement of heavy equipment and construction materials in Vietnam as the government promotes infrastructure development.[205]

Several Large Global 3PL Firms Provide Logistics Services in Vietnam

As noted, several large logistics firms currently operate in Vietnam, including global providers DHL, FedEx, TNT, and UPS. Other well-known firms that have established a presence in Vietnam include APL Logistics (Singapore), DB Schenker Logistics (Germany), Kuehne + Nagel, Maersk Logistics (Denmark), Nippon Express (Japan), and Panalpina (Switzerland). At least two government-owned entities also provide logistics services in Vietnam: Vinatrans, an integrated logistics services provider, and Vietnam Post and Telecommunications Group (VNPT), which serves the express delivery market.[206] Among global logistics firms, DHL has the most extensive operations in Vietnam, with 30 facilities around the country.[207] In 2009, DHL announced plans to invest an additional $10 million in Vietnam and create a joint venture with Vietnamese provider Oriental Logistics. The new firm, DHL Global Forwarding (Vietnam), will offer end-to-end logistics services, including freight forwarding, multimodal transport, warehousing and storage, and customs clearance.[208] Other global logistics firms in Vietnam have focused on niche markets. For example, in 2009, Panalpina opened a satellite office in southern Vietnam to serve the oil and gas industry.[209] Also in 2009, German firm DB Schenker opened a new logistics center near Ho Chi Minh City to provide services to original equipment manufacturers and contract manufacturers located in a nearby industrial park.[210] APL Logistics and Maersk Logistics, both affiliated with global maritime shipping firms, operate container storage and warehousing facilities at Vietnamese ports and provide freight forwarding and supply chain management services to customers in Vietnam.[211] In contrast to foreign 3PLs, the operations of domestic logistics firms are limited in scope and often focus on discrete areas of the logistics supply chain. For instance, while Vietnamese firm Ngoc Quang Services supplies air freight transport, another firm, Overseas Transport Company, functions primarily as a freight forwarder, and another, Cuchi Shipping, specializes in warehousing and in moving heavy freight.[212] The increasing number of partnerships between Vietnamese and foreign logistics firms may be one way for the former to build expertise in providing integrated logistics services. For example, UPS has formed a joint venture with Vietnamese logistics firm P&T Express, a subsidiary of VNPT. The new firm, UPS Vietnam, will expand the number of locations where UPS, working with its joint venture partner, can supply a full range of transportation and logistics services.[213]

Vietnam's Participation in the Global Logistics Market is Expanding

Vietnam has a limited but growing role in the international trade in logistics services. In 2008, Vietnam exported $7 billion in transportation services (used here as a proxy for logistics services) and imported $8 billion in such services.[214] These numbers represented 3 percent and 2 percent, respectively, of total Asian exports and imports of transportation services during that year, and less than 1 percent each of global exports and imports.[215] However, in 2008, Vietnamese exports in this sector increased by 25 percent over the previous year (compared to 15 percent for all Asian countries combined), while imports grew by 22 percent (compared to 18 percent for Asia). Overall, between 2005 and 2008, Vietnamese transportation services exports grew at a robust average annual rate of 18 percent, while imports rose by 21 percent.[216] Trade in freight transportation and logistics services is driven principally by merchandise trade. Hence the countries with which Vietnam conducts the most goods trade are the leading markets for Vietnamese exports and imports of transportation services (mainly air and maritime transport services).[217] In 2008, Vietnam's top three export markets for transportation services were the United States (which accounted for 19 percent of such exports), Japan (14 percent), and China (8 percent).[218] Within the Association of Southeast Asian Nations (ASEAN), Singapore, Malaysia, and the Philippines were the top markets for Vietnamese transportation services exports, collectively accounting for 10 percent of such exports in 2008.[219]

By contrast, 80 percent of Vietnamese transportation services imports come from neighboring Asian countries, including ASEAN members. A high volume of Vietnam's merchandise imports from Asian countries are reportedly transported by ship, spurring demand for Vietnamese imports of ocean freight services.[220]

Vietnam has Significantly Liberalized Its Logistics Services Sector

The Vietnamese government has launched several initiatives to widen access to its logistics sector and enhance its participation in the global logistics market. Under the General Agreement on Trade in Services (GATS) following its accession to the WTO in 2007, Vietnam made commitments in several areas related to logistics services, including courier services; express delivery services; and air, sea, road, and rail transportation services. For courier services, including express delivery, Vietnam currently caps foreign ownership in joint ventures at 51 percent. However, joint venture requirements in courier services are scheduled to be phased out by 2012, at which time 100 percent foreign ownership of Vietnamese courier and express delivery firms will be permitted.[221]

Vietnam's present commitments on air,[222] sea, road, and rail transportation services similarly place joint venture requirements on foreign providers, but for certain services such requirements will be eliminated after four to seven years from the date of Vietnam's WTO accession. Those include sea, road, and rail freight services; customs clearance services; container station and depot services; maintenance and repair of aircraft; and storage and warehousing.[223]

Vietnam is currently involved in an ASEAN-wide plan to integrate certain strategic sectors, including logistics. The plan recognizes logistics as an important driver of economic growth in the ASEAN region, and calls for the development of a single customs window among ASEAN countries as well as policies that will encourage private sector investment in logistics.[224] Vietnam intends to complete its part of the single customs window in 2012.[225]

Separately, Vietnam is one of six countries in the Greater Mekong Subregion participating in a program to improve cross-border transportation connectivity. The strengthening of transportation linkages among member countries is expected to increase cross-border trade and investment within the region. Among other outcomes, this program aims to improve rail connectivity between Vietnam, Cambodia, China, and Laos.[226]

Additionally, Vietnam has opened its aviation market to greater foreign participation, most recently by signing the ASEAN Multilateral Agreement on the Full Liberalization of Air Freight Services, which took effect in 2010.[227] This agreement, together with a similar one on air passenger services, establishes an open aviation area[228] in which airlines from signatory countries are permitted to provide unlimited service to, from, and within each other's markets.[229]

Overall, Vietnam has concluded more than 70 bilateral air service agreements with foreign countries, including an "open skies," or fully liberalized, agreement on air cargo services with the United States in 2008.[230] This agreement allowed U.S. logistics firms such as FedEx to expand air freight services between Vietnam and its trading partners.[231]

References

APL and Frost & Sullivan. "Vietnam Transportation and Logistics: Challenges and Opportunities," 2007.

APM Terminals. "Deepwater Access Deemed Key to Vietnam Port Utilization," October 14, 2010. http://www.apmterminals.com/uploaded Files/corporate/Media Center/Press Releases/10 1014 Deep Water Vietnam Port Utilization Key.pdf.

Armstrong & Associates, Inc. "U.S. 3PL Market Size Estimates." Press release, 2009. http://www.3plogistics.com//3PLmarket.htm.

———. "Global 3PL & Logistics Outsourcing Strategy." Press release, 2011. http://www.3plogistics.com/3PLmarketGlobal.htm.

Asian Development Bank (ADB). "Connecting Greater Mekong Subregion Railways: A Strategic Framework," August 2010.

Association of Southeast Asian Nations (ASEAN). "ASEAN Framework Agreement for the Integration of Priority Sectors." Vientiane, November 29, 2004. http://www.aseansec.org/16659.htm.

———. "ASEAN Multilateral Agreement on the Full Liberalisation of Air Freight Services." Manila, May 20 2009." http://www.asean.org/ 22628. htm

Bangkok Post. "Transport Cost Cut Goal to Be Derailed," January 27, 2011. http://www.bangkokpost.com/news/transport/218414/transport-cost-cust-goal-to-be-derailed.

Binh, Mong. "CAAV Says Will Open Skies for Qualified Foreign Airlines." *Saigon Times Daily*, November 13, 2008. http://english.thesaigontimes.vn/ Home/ict/info-tech/2000/.

Bloomberg. "Maersk APM Terminals to Develop Container Terminal in Vietnam," July 21, 2008. http://www.bloomberg.com/apps/news?pid= 21070001&sid=a6bH0ha84NZc.

Business Advantage Vietnam. "Driven to Expansion," 2010.

———. "Logistics Providers Make New Investments," 2010.

China Intelligence Online (CIO). "Vietnam—Air Transport and Infrastructure," September 23, 2010. http://www.chinaintelligenceonline. com/News/2010/09/23/vietnam-airline-update/.

———. "Vietnam—Port Development Brief," December 3, 2009. http://www.chinaintelligenceonline.com/News/2009/12/03/vietnam-port-development-brief/.

———. "Vietnam—Road Development Brief," January 8, 2010. http://www.chinaintelligenceonline.com/News/2010/01/08/vietnam-road-development-brief/.

———. "Vietnam—The Increasing Presence of DHL in Vietnam," November 19, 2009. http://www.chinaintelligenceonline.com/News/2009/11/19/the-increasing-presence-of-dhl-invietnam/.

CIA "Vietnam." *World Factbook*, updated March 8, 2011. http://www.cia.gov/library/publications/theworld-factbook/geos/vm.html.

Cuchi Shipping Company. "Introduction." http://www.cuchishipping.com/index.php?act=introduction (accessed March 28, 2011).

D.B. Schenker. "Schenker Vietnam." http://www.dbschenker.vn/?act=news_detail&id=54&lang (accessed March 7, 2011).

DHL. "DHL Invests Ahead of the Curve with US$10 Million Investment in Vietnam," June 23, 2009. http://www.dhl-dgf.com/press/2009/0623.html.

FedEx. "New FedEx Flight from Hanoi Improves Transit Time for Outbound Shipments." Press release, November 18, 2010. http://news.van.fedex.com/intl/cn?node=17018.

Government of Vietnam. General Statistics Office (GSO). "Some Main Indicators on Capacity of Transportation," 2008. http://www.gso.gov.vn/defaulten.aspx?tabid=473&idmid=3&ItemID= 10435.

———. GSO. "Volume of Freight by Type of Transport," n.d. http://www.gso.gov.vn/default_en.aspx?tabid=473&idmid=3&ItemID=10420 (accessed March 15, 2011).

———. GSO. "Volume of Freight by Transport Sector," n.d., http://www.gso.gov.vn/default_en.aspx?tabid=473&idmid=3&ItemID=10418 (accessed March 15, 2011).

———. Ministry of Planning and Investment (MPI). "Services Sector Development: A Key to Vietnam's Sustainable Growth," November 2005.

———. MPI. "Vietnam's IPs, EPZs and EZs: Ideal Places for Manufacturing Base," June 2007.

Global Express Association (GEA). "Vietnam." Customs Capabilities Reports, November 20, 2009. http://www.global-express.org/doc/Vietnam.pdf.

Global News. "Nippon Express Augments Logistics Services in Vietnam," March 16, 2010. http://www.nipponexpress.com/news/global/2010/16-Mar-10.html.

Hutchison Port Holdings. "Saigon International Terminals Vietnam." http://www.hph.com/globalbusiness/business.aspx?prt=prtver&sid=Introduction&gid=12 1 (accessed March 16, 2011).

International Labour Organization (ILO). *Vietnam Employment Trends*, 2010.

InterVISTAS-EU Consulting, Inc. *The Impact of International Air Service Liberalisation on Vietnam,* July 2009. http://www.iata.org/SiteCollectionDocuments/Documents/VietnamReport.pdf.

Johnson, Eric. "Vietnam on the Verge." *American Shipper*, December 2007. http://www.business-inasia.com/news/jan2009 news.html.

Kuehne + Nagel. "Heavy Lift Express in Vietnam." http://www.kn-portal.com/fileadmin/user upload/documents/seafreigh t/documents/Heavy lift express in Vietna m.pdf (accessed March 24, 2011).

Lee, Don. "Multinationals Take a Longer View of Vietnam." *Los Angeles Times*, April 11, 2009. http://articles.latimes.com/print/2009/apr/11/business/fi-vietnam11.

Organisation for Economic Co-operation and Development (OECD). "Transport Logistics: Shared Solutions to Common Challenges," 2002.

Panalpina. "Annual Report 2009," 2009. http://www.panalpina.com/content/www/global/en/home/investor_relations/annual_report/_jcr_content/contentParSys/download0/downloadList/ 2009.spooler.download/panalpina ar09 web co mplete small.pdf.

Putzger, Ian. "Bullish Integrators Step Up Asia Flights." *eCargonews Asia*, June 7, 2010. http://www.cargonewsasia.com/secured/ article.aspx?article=22860.

Saigon Newport Holding Company. "Deep-water Ports and the Supporting Logistics Network." Presentation at the American Chamber of Commerce in Vietnam, August 2009. http://www.amchamvietnam.com/download/1267/L2Rvd25sb2FkLzEyNjc.

Supply Chain Management. "Vietnam: Lack of Logistics Infrastructure = Higher Logistics Costs," September 25, 2008. http://www.3plwire.com/2008/09/2/vietnam-lack-of-logistics-infrastructurehigher-logistics-costs/print/.

Transport Intelligence. *Vietnam Logistics 2009*. February 2009.

United Nations Commodity Trade Statistics Database (Comtrade). "Viet Nam." http://comtrade.un.org (accessed March 9, 2011).

United Nations Conference on Trade and Development (UNCTAD). *Investment Policy Review: Viet Nam*. (United Nations: New York and Geneva), 2008.

United Nations Economic Commission for Europe. "The Single Window Concept," April 2003. http://unpan1.un.org/intradoc/groups/public/documents/UNECE/UNPAN019892.pdf.

United Nations Statistics Division. United Nations Service Trade database. 2010. http://unstats.un.org/unsd/servicetrade/default.aspx (accessed March 8, 2011).

United States International Trade Commission (USITC). *Logistic Services: An Overview of the Global Market and Potential Effects of Removing Trade Impediments*. USITC Publication 3770. Washington, DC: USITC, May 2005.

Viet NamNet Bridge. "Vietnam Works to Gain Market Share in Logistics Services," September 11, 2007. http://english.vietnamnet.vn/biz/2007/11/754021.

———. "What's the Aviation Market in the WTO Period Like?" *Viet NamNet Bridge*, December 21, 2006. http://english.vietnamnet.vn/biz/2006/12/646253/.

Vietnam Business Forum. "Logistics Integration: Driving Force for ASEAN Economic Development," September 7, 2010. http://www.vccinews.com/news detail.asp?news id=21528.

Vietnam Business News. "High-Tech Multinationals Invest in VN," September 28, 2010. http://vietnambusiness.asia/high-tech-multinationals-invest-in-vn/.

———. "TNT Vietnam Expands Logistics Capacity," January 23, 2010.

Vietnam Business & Economy News. "A Fresh Start for Infrastructure Investment," January 17, 2011. http://www.vneconomynews.com/ 2011/01/fresh-start-for-infrastructure.html.

World Bank. *Doing Business 2011*. Washington, DC: World Bank, 2011. http://www.doingbusiness.org/~/media/FPDKM/Doing%20Business/Documents/Profiles/Country/ DB11/VNM.pdf.

World Trade Organization (WTO). "World Trade in Transportation Services by Region, 2008." http://www.wto.org/english/res e/statis e/its2009 e/section3 e/iii03.xls (accessed April 6, 2011).

———. "Leading Exporters and Importers of Transportation Services, 2008." http://www.wto.org/english/res e/statis e/its2009 e/section3 e/iii04.xls (accessed April 6, 2011).

———. "Working Party on the Accession of Viet Nam." WT/ACC/VNM/48/Add.2. October 27, 2006. http://docsonline.wto.org/DDFDocuments/t/wt/acc/vnm48a2.doc

———. Statistical Division. "Country Profiles: Vietnam," October 2010. http://stat.wto.org/CountryProfiles/VN e/htm.

RETAIL SERVICES

Retailing is the final step in the distribution of merchandise to consumers. Retailers purchase their products from manufacturers, agricultural producers, or wholesalers, then sell these goods in small quantities to consumers. Retailers may use fixed points of sale (i.e., physical stores), or nonstore channels (such as catalogs, Web sites, and door-to-door solicitation). In addition to selling merchandise, retailers may offer services associated with the merchandise (for example, appliance installation and repair).[232]

Vietnam's retail industry is growing rapidly and is an important source of jobs and output in the Vietnamese economy. Retail sales totaled $45.7 billion in 2010, up from $27.1 billion in 2006. Together with wholesale trading and repair services, it accounted for 11.0 percent of employment and 14.8 percent of gross domestic product in 2009.[233]

Before the *Đổi Mới* economic reforms that began in 1986,[234] food was distributed by the state via a ration coupon system and most private retail trading was banned (though it never disappeared entirely).[235] After the reforms, small, family-owned shops and traditional bazaars quickly multiplied and became the dominant channels for retail trade. Today, Vietnam has nearly one million family-owned shops, over 8,000 bazaars, and a large informal retail industry. More than 85 percent of product distribution in Vietnam occurs through such traditional retail channels.[236] Modern outlets such as supermarkets, department stores, and similar outlets are becoming increasingly numerous, but it is unclear whether these outlets will supplant traditional retailers.[237]

Vietnam's Consumers are Spending More and Buying More Discretionary Items

Vietnam's consumers have spent more as they have grown wealthier. Between 2006 and 2010, annual consumer spending per capita increased from $446 to $741, an increase of 66.1 percent.[238] Over the same period, the share of spending on groceries dropped from 46.1 percent to 43.0 percent, while the share devoted to electronics, entertainment, and personal office supplies grew from 6.4 percent to 7.0 percent.[239] These data suggest that Vietnamese shoppers are gradually devoting a smaller share of their spending to essentials and more to discretionary items. While this pattern is not uncommon in developing countries, observers have described an unusually rapid "leapfrogging" by Vietnamese consumers into sophisticated products. For example, one foreign-owned distributor of laundry detergents noted that the firm's largest-selling item was powdered soaps for traditional, labor-intensive hand washing, but the fastest-growing item was fabric softener (a product that generally requires a washing machine or dryer).[240] Sales of luxury goods are also increasing rapidly, albeit from a small base.[241]

Demand for Modern Retail Formats Is Increasing

Vietnam's increasingly affluent consumers value the cleanliness, relatively broad product ranges, environmental amenities (such as air conditioning), and fixed prices that are characteristic of modern stores.[242] In 1995, there were 10 supermarkets and two modern shopping centers in Vietnam; by 2010, there were an estimated 750 supermarkets and hypermarkets and 150 shopping centers and department stores.[243] Over the same period, modern grocery sales increased from $1.6 billion to $6.7 billion.[244]

Despite this growth, modern retailers continue to face significant competition from traditional merchants. Vietnam's poor rarely shop at supermarkets because they perceive them as inaccessible and expensive, and because the stores are not as likely as traditional merchants to let them buy on credit.[245] While poverty has declined rapidly in recent years, the poor are still a large segment of Vietnam's consumers—as recently as 2008 almost 40 percent of Vietnamese lived on incomes of less than $2 per day.[246] Furthermore, even wealthier Vietnamese often prefer to buy certain types of merchandise from traditional markets, especially fresh produce. Consumers view the produce at traditional markets as fresher than that in modern supermarkets, and they consider traditional markets convenient and competitively priced.[247]

Complex Regulations Slow the Entry of Foreign Firms

When Vietnam acceded to the WTO in January 2007, it committed to phase out equity caps for retailing by January 2008 and joint venture requirements by January 2009, and to allow foreign firms to trade in "all legally imported and domestically produced products" beginning in January 2010.[248] However, Vietnam kept a requirement that foreign-owned retailers pass an economic needs test (ENT) in order to set up outlets beyond their first store.[249] Vietnam's GATS schedule states that the ENT should be administered following "pre-established publicly available procedures" using objective criteria.[250] Vietnam has passed two regulations that list the ENT criteria, but the regulations do not explain how regulators will apply them. For example, one of the criteria is "market stability," but the regulations do not define market stability or explain how regulators will decide whether a market is stable. Moreover, the regulations assign most license-issuing responsibilities to provincial authorities, but these authorities may not issue the licenses without approval from the Ministry of Industry and Trade (MOIT), and the regulations do not state whether MOIT imposes conditions for such approvals beyond the ENT criteria.[251]

The ENT is regularly described as an instrument to shield domestic retailers from foreign competition.[252] For example, in January 2009, an official of the MOIT sought to assuage domestic retailers' fear of foreign competition by noting the difficulty of satisfying the ENT.[253] Some observers have suggested that the opaque nature of the ENT procedures discourages major foreign retailers, including U.S. firms, from pursuing investments in Vietnam,[254] and that it affects the operations and growth of foreign-invested firms already in Vietnam. For example, South Korea's Lotte Shopping, which operates in Vietnam via a joint venture, saw its plan for a second shopping center in Ho Chi Minh City rejected by the city's Department of Planning and Investment in 2009. This rejection has affected the company's plans for rapid expansion within Vietnam.[255]

Poor Logistics are Hobbling the Development of Distribution Networks

Efficient customs procedures, sound transport infrastructure, and competitive logistic services enable retailers to move their merchandise reliably and cost-effectively. Vietnam has improved in these areas in recent years[256] but continues to face challenges. Out of 155 countries included in the World Bank's 2010 Logistics Performance Index, Vietnam ranked 51st in competence and quality of logistics service providers, 53rd in efficiency of customs clearance, and 66th in quality of trade and transport related infrastructure (see the "Logistics Services" section).[257] Infrastructure tends to be better in cities than in rural areas,[258] which has contributed to the concentration of modern retail outlets in the major urban centers. Ho Chi Minh

City has led growth in modern retail, followed by Hanoi. Danang and Can Tho, two other large cities, have also seen substantial retail development.[259]

Firms Face a Shortage of Talented Managers

Vietnam has a shortage of local personnel trained for middle or upper management positions, which impacts retailing as well as other industries.[260] One government official notes that education relating to distribution systems is not commonly provided by Vietnam's education system: "Nobody has been trained in how to operate a warehouse, how to merchandise, how to operate a store, how to manage logistics, or how to manage chain stores."[261] Vietnam has asked international organizations and developed countries for help with training in these areas (see the "Education Services" section).[262]

This scarcity of skilled retail managers makes it difficult for retailers to apply cutting-edge operational and management practices, such as using point-of-sale data to fine-tune their inventory, marketing, and pricing strategies. The shortage of management skills is particularly acute for domestically owned retailers, who do not have the built-in access to foreign expertise that foreign-invested retailers enjoy.[263]

High Real Estate Prices Affect the Pace of Retail Development

In Vietnam, where the state owns all land and property for store locations must be leased, real estate is among retailers' highest costs.[264] Prices in the central business districts of Ho Chi Minh City and Hanoi are especially high: at the most expensive shopping location in Ho Chi Minh City, yearly rent was $323 per square foot in 2010, higher than the most expensive locations in Singapore ($317), Toronto ($295), and Amsterdam ($261).[265]

These prices reflect the shortage of high-quality retail space in Hanoi and Ho Chi Minh City.[266] However, supply is expanding in response to growing demand; for example, in Hanoi the supply of retail floor space quadrupled from 2005 to 2010.

Several new shopping centers in Hanoi were nearing completion in 2011, and operators of some shopping centers were offering substantial discounts to attract and retain tenants.[267]

Half of Vietnam's Top 10 Retailers are Foreign-Owned

Among Vietnam's top 10 retailers, all but 2 derive the majority of their sales from groceries, and 5 of the 10 are foreign-owned (table 4). Such dominance of the retail market by grocers is common in many countries. Supermarkets and other stores selling everyday goods (e.g., hypermarkets and superstores) tend to be high-volume businesses, and the list of leading retailers worldwide is topped by such firms.

Table 4. Top 10 retailers in Vietnam, 2010

Company	Country	Sales ($ million)	Grocery[(a)] share of sales (%)	Number of establishments
Saigon Co-op	Vietnam	622.6	66.9	60
Metro Group	Germany	596.3	66.4	13
Casino	France	337.4	51.8	14
LVMH	France	177.5	28.3	6
Fivimart	Vietnam	141.0	84.4	15
G7	Vietnam	89.9	88.4	460
Maximark	Vietnam	83.2	66.8	6
Citimart	Vietnam	64.8	84.4	21
Lotte Shopping	South Korea	52.2	51.0	2
Parkson Corp	Malaysia	39.8	12.8	8

Source: Planet Retail database (accessed April 11, 2011)

Notes: [a]Planet Retail defines groceries as "virtually everything one would find in a standard supermarket, comprising fruit & vegetables, chilled, frozen, ambient, alcoholic drinks, non-alcoholic drinks, tobacco, pet care and household care."

The world's two leading foreign-invested retailers entered Vietnam before the country's 2007 accession to the WTO: France's Groupe Bourbon (now Groupe Casino) entered via a joint venture with local partners in 1998,[268] while Germany's Metro Group established a wholly owned subsidiary in 2002.[269] Foreign-owned firms once focused almost exclusively on serving Vietnam's main urban centers, but a few have recently ventured into less populated areas.[270] Their motivation to enter these areas is twofold: demand for modern retail is underserved in these areas, and it is becoming more difficult to expand in large cities due to regulatory hurdles and the scarcity of suitable real estate.[271] A number of other foreign retailers have recently launched joint ventures with Vietnamese companies to serve the Vietnamese market. For example, in December 2010, Japan's Ministop entered a joint venture with G7 to create a convenience store chain,[272] and Singapore's NTUC Fair Price established a joint venture with Saigon Co-op to create a new chain of hypermarkets.

The Vietnamese government owns the two leading domestically owned retailers, Saigon Co-op and Fivimart.[273] No Vietnam-owned retailers currently operate outside of Vietnam, although Saigon Coop has announced its intention to enter Cambodia in the near future.[274]

References

Breu, Marco, Brian S. Salsberg, and Hà Thanh Tú. "Growing Up Fast: Vietnam Discovers the Consumer Society." *McKinsey Quarterly*, August 2010. http://www.mckinseyquarterly.com/Marketing/Sales Distribution/ Growing up fast Vietnam dis covers the consumer society 2655?gp=1 (registration required).

Cason, Timothy N., Daniel Friedman, and Garrett H. Milam. "Bargaining versus Posted Price Competition in Customer Markets." *International Journal of Industrial Organization* 21, no. 2 (February 2003), 223–51.

Cushman & Wakefield. "Hanoi Retail Report, 1Q11." Hanoi: Cushman & Wakefield, April 12, 2011. http://www.cushwake.com/cwmbs1q11/ pdf/hanoi retail 1q11.pdf.

———. *Main Streets across the World 2010*. London: Cushman & Wakefield, 2010. http://www.cushwake.com/cwglobal/jsp/kcReportDetail.jsp?Country=GL OBAL&Language=EN &catId=100003&pId=c31300002p.

Figuié, Muriel, and Paule Moustier. "Market Appeal in an Emerging Economy: Supermarkets and Poor Consumers in Vietnam." *Food Policy* 34, no. 2 (April 2009): 210–17. http://www.sciencedirect.com/science/ article/ pii/S0306919208000961 (subscription required).

Government of Vietnam. General Statistics Office (GSO). "Structure of Employed Population at 15 Years of Age and Above as of Annual 1 July by Types of Ownership and Kinds of Economic Activity." n.d. (accessed April 7, 2011).

———. GSO. "Structure of Gross Domestic Product at Current Prices by Ownership and by Kind of Economic Activity." n.d. http://www.gso.gov. vn/defaulten.aspx?tabid=468&idmid=3&ItemID =9907 (accessed April 13, 2011).

Hung, Quoc. "Plan for Second Lotte Mart in City Rejected." *Saigon Times Daily*, May 6, 2009. http://english.thesaigontimes.vn/Home/ sports/home/ 4337/.

International Monetary Fund (IMF). World Economic Outlook database, April 2011.
http://www.imf.org/external/pubs/ft/weo/2011/01/weodata/index.aspx (accessed April 12, 2011).

Maruyama, Masayoshi, and Le Viet Trung. "Modern Retailers in Transition Economies: The Case of Vietnam." Kobe University, Research Institute for Economics and Business Administration, Discussion Paper Series DP 2011–08, March 10, 2011. http://www.rieb.kobeu.ac.jp/academic/ra/dp/ English/DP2011-08.pdf.

———. "Traditional Bazaar or Supermarkets: A Probit Analysis of Affluent Consumer Perceptions in Hanoi." *International Review of Retail, Distribution and Consumer Research* 17, no. 3 (233–52): July 2007. http://www.tandfonline.com/doi/abs/10.1080/09593960701368804#previe w (subscription required).

McKinsey & Company. "Understanding the New Vietnam." Video, June 2010. http://csi.mckinsey.com/en/Knowledge by region/Asia/Rest of Asia/Growing up fast.aspx.

Metro Cash & Carry Vietnam. "Background and History."
http://www.metro.com.vn/servlet/PB/menu/1108611 l2/index.html (accessed September 12, 2011).

Nguyen, Xuan Thanh, and David Dapice. "Vietnam's Infrastructure Constraints." UNDP-Harvard Policy Dialogue Papers, Series on Vietnam's WTO Accession and International Competitiveness Research, Policy Dialogue Paper No. 3, 2009. http://www.innovations.harvard.edu/ cache/documents/6533/653317.pdf.

Phan Thi, Giac Tam. "Poor Consumers' Access to Supermarkets in Ho Chi Minh City." In *Supermarkets and the Poor in Vietnam,* edited by Paule Moustier, The Anh Dao, Bang An Hoang, Binh Vu Trong, Muriel Figuié, Giac Tam Phan Thi, and Tan Loc Nguyen Thi. Hanoi: Cartographic Publishing House, 2006. Cited in Muriel Figuié and Paule Moustier, "Market Appeal in an Emerging Economy: Supermarkets and Poor Consumers in Vietnam." *Food Policy* 34, no. 2 (April 2009): 210–17. http://www.sciencedirect.com/science/article/pii/S0306919208000961 (subscription required).

Planet Retail. "Country Report: Vietnam," April 6, 2011. www.planetretail.net (subscription required).

———. "New Dawn for Vietnam's Retail Sector," January 9, 2009. www.planetretail.net (subscription required).

———. Planet Retail database. www.planetretail.net (accessed various dates) (subscription required).

Reardon, Thomas, and Ashok Gulati. "The Supermarket Revolution in Developing Countries." IFPRI Policy Brief 2, June 2008. http://ageconsearch.umn.edu/bitstream/47660/2/bp002.pdf.

Reardon, Thomas, C. Peter Timmer, Christopher B. Barrett, and Julio Berdegué. "The Rise of Supermarkets in Africa, Asia and Latin America." *American Journal of Agricultural Economics* 85, no. 5 (December 2003): 1140–6.

Saigon Co.op Mart. "History." n.d. (accessed April 13, 2011).

U.S. Agency for International Development (USAID) and Vietnam Competitiveness Initiative (VNCI). "Vietnam Provincial Competitiveness Index 2009." Hanoi: USAID and VNCI, 2009. http://www.vnci.org/sites/default/files/VNCI No14 PCI%202009%20report%20EN final.pdf.

U.S. Census Bureau. "2007 NAICS Definition: Sector 44–45; Retail Trade," 2007. http://www.census.gov/cgi-bin/sssd/naics/naicsrch?code=44&search=2007%20NAICS%20Search.

Việt Nam News (VNS). "Domestic Distributors Need Not Be Afraid." *VietNamNet Bridge,* January 3, 2009. http://english.vietnamnet.vn/biz/2009/01/821966/.

VietNamNet Bridge. "Retailers Following 'Expansionism' in Vietnam's Market," March 4, 2011. http://www.itpc.gov.vn/importers/news/2011-01-04.148333/03/2011-03- 04.965788/MISNews view?b start:int=20&set language=en.

VietNamNet Bridge. "Saigon Co.op Touches on Shopping Mall," March 9, 2010.
http://www.vca.org.vn/Default.aspx?tabid=163&News=2159&CategoryID=19.

World Bank. Investing Across Borders database. http://iab.worldbank.org (accessed July 21, 2011).

———. "2010 Logistics Performance Index," 2010. http://info.worldbank.org/etools/tradesurvey/mode1a.asp?countryID=153 (accessed April 8, 2011).

———. World Development Indicators database. http://data.worldbank.org/indicator (accessed July 15, 2011).

World Trade Organization (WTO). "Viet Nam: Schedule of Specific Commitments." GATS/SC/142, March 19, 2007. www.wto.org.

Wrigley, Neil, and Michelle Lowe. "The Globalization of Trade in Retail Services." Report commissioned by the Organisation for Economic Co-operation and Development (OECD) Trade Policy Linkages and Services Division for the OECD Experts Meeting on Distribution Services. Paris: OECD, November 17, 2010. http://www.oecd.org/document/33/0,3746,en 2649 36344374 46259617 1 1 1 1,00.html.

TELECOMMUNICATIONS SERVICES

Over the past several years, strong economic growth in Vietnam and liberalization efforts by the government have led to rapid growth in the country's telecommunication services market.

Between 2000 and 2009, the total number of telephone subscriptions grew from 2.4 million to roughly 116 million,[275] for a compound annual growth rate of 47 percent.

Growth in total telecommunication subscribers was driven by both mobile services, which grew at an annual rate of 77 percent, and fixed-line services, which grew at an annual rate of 24 percent.[276]

The number of telecommunication subscribers is expected to continue to grow over the next five years, albeit at declining rates due to the increasing saturation of both fixed-line and mobile markets.[277]

The Vietnamese telecommunication services market, measured by revenues of fixed-line, mobile, and Internet services, was valued at $4.7 billion at the end of 2009, reflecting an annual growth rate of 28 percent since 2006. Mobile services were by far the largest segment, accounting for 86 percent of total revenues; the fixed-line and Internet markets accounted for 6 and 8 percent respectively.

Driven by strong subscriber growth, revenues in the mobile segment grew by 38 percent annually during 2006–09 and were the primary driver of growth in the overall telecommunication services market.

Although revenues in the Internet market grew at an annual rate of 49 percent during this period, they accounted for a small share of total revenues and thus had a relatively small influence on overall growth rates. Revenues in the fixed-line market declined 51 percent, from $600 million in 2006 to $290 million by the end of 2009.[278]

Telecommunications Have Been Liberalized but Remain Heavily Regulated

The Vietnamese telecommunication services market has experienced substantial liberalization over the past 10 years, though it remains heavily regulated by the state. This liberalization has been steady but slow, often including public announcements supporting reform followed by ineffective action.[279] This ambivalent approach stems from the fact that Vietnam's centralized government remains focused on maintaining control over strategic parts of the economy, including telecommunication services. While reformers in Vietnam support liberalization and deregulation, opposing constituencies are concerned about the social, political, and financial consequences of liberalization.[280]

Vietnam's telecommunication services market is regulated by the Ministry of Information and Communications (MIC), which replaced the Ministry of Posts and Telematics as the country's main telecommunication services regulator in 2007.[281] The MIC has numerous and broad responsibilities: it is the policy-making and regulatory body for telecommunication and Internet services; data transmission; information, technology, and electronics; network infrastructure; and radio frequency management.[282] The MIC's main functions include drafting laws, ordinances, regulations, strategies, and development plans pertaining to telecommunications and information technologies. Other responsibilities include regulating investment in the telecommunications sector; granting and revoking telecommunication licenses; regulating numbering resources, codes, domain names, and Internet addresses; and guiding and planning activities related to national radio frequency spectrum.[283]

In November 2009, the National Assembly passed the Law on Telecommunications (Telecom Law) and the Law on Radiofrequency, which overhauled telecommunication regulation to promote investment and bring Vietnam in line with its WTO accession commitments.[284] The Telecom Law encouraged networks to share infrastructure, established access and interconnection obligations on companies owning essential network facilities, reduced restrictions on private ownership in facilities-based service providers, and set up an open and transparent process for granting telecommunication licenses.[285] The Telecom Law also created a new regulatory body, the Vietnam Telecommunications Authority (VNTA), an assisting agency to the MIC.[286] In June 2011, implementing legislation tasked the VNTA with regulating telecommunication infrastructure, interconnection, tariffs, promotions, and service quality; promoting competition; facilitating universal service obligations; and settling disputes between carriers.[287]

Vietnam's telecom and radio frequency laws, which came into effect in July 2010 and are currently being implemented, clarify business conditions in the country's telecommunication sector. For example, Decree 25[288] provides guidelines for the cross-ownership and foreign investment provisions of the Telecom Law. Among other issues, it stipulates that any enterprise owning more than 20 percent of the charter capital or shares in one telecommunication enterprise cannot concurrently own more than 20 percent of the charter capital or shares in another enterprise that provides the same service in the same market.[289] Decree 25 also establishes capital and investment requirements for fixed-line, mobile, and satellite networks, ranging from $250,000 to $24 million (depending on network type, coverage, and subscriber numbers). Within three years of licensing, all networks require a minimum investment of three times the required capital. Services using radio spectrum require higher commitments, ranging from $48 million to $360 million over 15 years. Decree 25 also covers licensing and investment procedures, dispute settlements, infrastructure sharing, and treatment of subscriber information.[290]

Vietnam's Telecommunication Sector Has Gradually Become More Open to Foreign Investors

For many years, regulations disadvantaged foreign operators and discouraged foreign investment in Vietnam's telecommunications sector.[291] Until 2005, there was a total prohibition on foreign ownership of telecommunications companies and networks. Foreign companies that wanted to enter the telecommunication services market were required to use a legal structure called a business cooperation contract (BCC). Under the terms of a typical BCC, a foreign operator would partner with a government-controlled telecommunication operator, with the foreign operator providing equipment, financing, and technical services, and the incumbent managing network operations. BCC partners would share revenues based upon a negotiated formula for 5 to 15 years.[292] Most of the foreign operators currently in Vietnam, including France Telecom, Korea Telecom, NTT (Japan), and Telestra (Australia), entered the market via BCC arrangements.[293]

Over time, foreign companies became dissatisfied with their lack of operational control under BCCs, and many argued that the limited lifespan of a typical BCC encouraged short-term decision-making. As a result, foreign telecommunication companies began to lobby the Vietnamese government for better alternatives. Concerned about the country's ability to attract foreign investment in the telecommunication sector, the government passed legislation in 2005 that allowed foreign companies to convert their BCCs into joint ventures.[294] Currently, foreign carriers are allowed to enter into two types of joint ventures with Vietnamese operators: joint stock companies and multi-member limited liability corporations.[295] Although such arrangements increase the autonomy of foreign firms, some observers note that the legal mechanisms for converting BCCs to joint ventures are incomplete; for example, it is not clear whether a BCC's telecommunication service license automatically transfers to a new joint venture entity.[296]

International agreements have also facilitated foreign investment in the Vietnamese telecom sector. Under the 2001 U.S.-Vietnam BTA, Vietnam agreed to observe the principles of the WTO's Basic Telecommunications Reference Paper and accepted additional commitments on basic and value-added services. For example, U.S. companies were allowed to form joint ventures with Vietnamese telecommunication service companies after a grace period of two to six years, although foreign equity was capped at 49 percent in voice telephone services[297] and basic telecommunication services,[298] and at 50 percent in value-added services.[299] Vietnam undertook similar commitments on telecommunication services as part of its accession to the WTO in 2007.[300]

The Fixed-Line Market in Vietnam Has Gained Subscribers While Losing Revenue

Unlike in many countries, the number of fixed-line subscribers in Vietnam has grown robustly over the past few years.[301] From 2006 through 2009, subscribers grew by 27 percent annually. By the end of 2009, Vietnam had more than 17 million fixed-line subscribers, representing a penetration rate of 20 percent, with most lines concentrated in Hanoi and Ho Chi Minh City.[302] By comparison, the average fixed-line penetration in economically comparable countries was only 8.6 percent in 2009.[303] Rapid growth over the past few years is attributable both to a low starting base and to the growth of broadband services (mainly in urban areas), which are delivered almost exclusively using fixed-line-based digital subscriber line (DSL) technologies. Vietnam's fixed-line infrastructure was so underdeveloped that ongoing construction has been necessary to connect thousands of rural communities throughout the country.[304] However, despite growth in subscribers, fixed-line revenue fell from 2006 to 2009 as competition with mobile services drove down prices.[305]

In October 2011, there were eight fixed-line telecommunication service providers licensed to operate in Vietnam, all which were either directly or indirectly controlled by government ministries. Nearly 100 percent of the fixed-line market is dominated by just four operators. The leading fixed-line operator is the state-owned incumbent, Vietnam Posts and Telecommunications (VNPT), which had 11 million fixed-line subscribers in 2009 (representing 63 percent of the market).[306] The other leading fixed-line operators are the Vietnamese Army-backed Viettel (with 22 percent market share), EVN Telecom (14 percent),[307] and Saigon Post and Telecommunications (1 percent).[308] Hanoi Telecom, the Corporation for Financing and Promoting Technology,[309] CMC Telecom, and GTel hold fixed-line licenses but have not achieved meaningful market share.[310] VNPT, Viettel, FPT, and EVN Telecom also hold licenses to offer international services.[311] Voice telephone services delivered using voice-over-Internet-protocol (VoIP) technologies are allowed in Vietnam and encouraged by the government. As of August 2011, eight companies held concessions to offer long-distance and international VoIP services.[312]

The Government Retains Ownership Stakes in All Mobile Services Providers

As in many developing countries, the Vietnamese mobile telephone services market has grown very rapidly in recent years. From 2006 through 2009, the number of mobile subscribers grew from about 19 million to 98 million, representing an annual growth rate of 73 percent. By the end of 2010, the mobile penetration rate stood at 113 percent, compared to 22.4 percent in 2006.[313] By contrast, the mobile penetration rate in countries of similar economic development was 57.3 percent.[314] While the Vietnamese mobile services sector has undoubtedly exhibited strong growth, subscriber numbers are likely inflated due to the fact that many Vietnamese consumers buy multiple subscriber identity module (SIM) cards[315] and quickly dispose of them after the credits are consumed. Indeed, in 2010, MIC estimated that only 75 percent of the nation's reported wireless subscribers were active subscribers. Given the competitiveness of the market, SIM card turnover is likely to remain high. In an effort to better calculate subscriber numbers, MIC announced in 2009 that consumers may own no more than three SIM cards from each operator.[316] The Vietnamese government owns direct or indirect stakes in all mobile service providers. Although eight mobile carriers are currently operating in Vietnam, nearly 90 percent of the market is controlled by three operators: Vietnamese Army-controlled Viettel (with a 34 percent market share in 2009) and two competing subsidiaries of VNPT, Vinafone (27 percent) and Mobifone (27 percent). Other companies offering mobile services in Vietnam include S-Telecom (5 percent market share),[317] Hanoi Telecom Co. (4 percent),[318] GTel Mobile (2 percent),[319] and EVN Telecom (1 percent).[320] The government of Vietnam has also licensed two mobile virtual network operators[321] to offer services in Vietnam: Indochina Telecom and Vietnam Multimedia Corporation. As of October 2011, neither firm had launched commercial services.[322] As part of its WTO commitments, the Vietnamese government plans to sell up to 49 percent of its various telecommunication holdings. Progress has been slow, however, and the government's efforts to privatize MobiFone and EVN Telecom were unsuccessful. Privatization activities are not expected to resume until 2013 at the earliest.[323]

There are many mobile services providers trying to gain share in a near-saturated market, driving fierce competition that largely revolves around prices. For example, in response to the entry of GTel in 2009, Viettel reduced its prices by one-third, prompting its rivals to also cut prices. In 2010, Viettel cut its per-minute prices by another 10–15 percent, and its competitors again cut prices in response. In an effort to end such price wars, Viettel, Vinaphone, and MobiFone agreed to refrain from cutting prices in 2011 and instead compete by focusing on niche markets and high-bandwidth third generation (3G) mobile services.[324]

Licenses for 3G mobile services were first issued in April 2009, and are held by Viettel, Vinaphone, and MobiFone as well as a Hanoi Telecom/EVN Telecom consortium.[325] By the end of 2010, approximately 7 percent of Vietnam's users had subscribed to 3G services.[326] The MIC recently awarded test licenses to build fourth generation (4G) networks to VNPT, FPT Telecom, VTC, CMC, and Viettel.[327] Commercial LTE services are expected to be launched in 2015, when spectrum currently used by television broadcasters is scheduled to be vacated.[328]

The Number of Internet Users Has Grown Rapidly

The number of Internet users in Vietnam rose dramatically from 200,000 in 2000 to 23 million in 2009, representing nearly 70 percent annual growth.[329]

Despite this growth, Internet penetration stood at only 27 percent at the end of 2009; constraints include limited network infrastructure outside urban areas and low per capita income, which makes it difficult for consumers to afford Internet service subscriptions and personal computers.[330] At the end of 2009, only about 20 percent of total Internet users received highspeed Internet services via DSL, cable television, leased-line, or fiber-to-the-home technologies.[331]

Vietnam has issued three types of licenses to companies offering Internet services: (1) the Internet Service Provider (ISP) license for providing retail Internet services; (2) the Internet Exchange Provider (IXP) license for providing wholesale bandwidth to ISPs; and (3) the Online Service Provider (OSP) license for providing Internet application services. As of August 2011, the MIC had issued 54 ISP licenses,[332] although more than 90 percent of the market is controlled by three companies: VNPT (69 percent market share in 2009), FPT (14 percent), and Viettel (9 percent).[333] The MIC had also licensed 11 IXP operators and issued 80 OSP concessions as of late 2010.[334]

References

Baker & McKenzie. Client Alert: Vietnam Issues Long-Awaited Decree Implementing Telecoms Law, April 2011.

Economist Intelligence Unit (EIU). Vietnam: Telecoms and Technology Report. London: Economist Intelligence Unit, June 16, 2011.

Hot Telecom. Country Profile: Vietnam. Montreal, Canada: Hot Telecom, May 2011. Indochine Counsel. Client Alert, April–May 2011.

International Telecommunications Union. ITU World Telecommunications /ICT Indicators 2010 database (access March 3, 2011).

LookAtVietnam. “Five Bills Adopted at NA Session,” November 24, 2009.

Government of Vietnam. Ministry of Information and Communication (MIC). Vietnam Information and Technology White Book 2010. Hanoi: Information and Communications Publishing House, 2010.

———. MIC. “Main Functions.” MIC Website (accessed September 12, 2011).

Paul Budde Communication Pty Ltd. Vietnam: Key Statistics, Telecommunications Market and Regulatory Overview, and Broadcasting. Bucketty, Australia: Paul Budde Communication Pty Ltd, August 3, 2011.

TeleGeography. Vietnam. Washington, DC: TeleGeography, August 31, 2011.

World Bank. World Development Indicators Online Database. http://databank.worldbank.org/ddp/home.do (accessed November 1, 2011).
World Trade Organization (WTO). "Working Party on the Accession of Viet Nam." WT/ACC/VNM/48/Add.2. October 27, 2006. http://docsonline.wto.org/DDFDocuments/t/wt/acc/vnm48a2.doc
U.S.-Vietnam Bilateral Trade Agreement. Annex G, Vietnam: Schedule of Specific Commitments of Trade in Services, 2001.

INTELLECTUAL PROPERTY RIGHTS

Vietnam's legal framework for intellectual property rights (IPR)[335] was overhauled during the last decade, partly to comply with its obligations under the WTO's Trade-Related Aspects of Intellectual Property Rights (TRIPS) Agreement.[336] As part of its WTO accession, the government of Vietnam restructured its IPR laws with a 2005 Civil Code and 2005 Intellectual Property Law.[337] Vietnam has implemented regulations and issued decrees to strengthen its IPR framework further in the years since this initial restructuring. For example, in 2009 the government increased fines and added criminal penalties for certain types of infringement.[338]

In addition to the TRIPS Agreement, Vietnam is a signatory to most major IPR conventions and treaties organized under the World Intellectual Property Organization (WIPO).[339] These include the Berne Convention for mutual recognition of copyrights (joined in 2004), the Madrid Protocol for mutual recognition of trademarks (2006), the Paris Union for industrial property protection (1949), and the Patent Cooperation Treaty for unified patent filing procedures (1993).[340] Outside the WIPO framework, Vietnam is a signatory to the International Convention for the Protection of New Varieties of Plants (2006).[341] Vietnam also made IPR commitments as part of the 2001 U.S.-Vietnam BTA.[342]

Three Vietnamese government ministries are responsible for IPR as defined in Vietnam's Intellectual Property Law.[343] The National Office of Intellectual Property (NOIP) manages patents and trademarks; the Copyright Office of Vietnam oversees copyrights and other creative IP; and the Office of New Plant Varieties Protection regulates new plant varieties (figure 6). These offices were created or changed in concert with Vietnam's preparation for its WTO accession.[344]

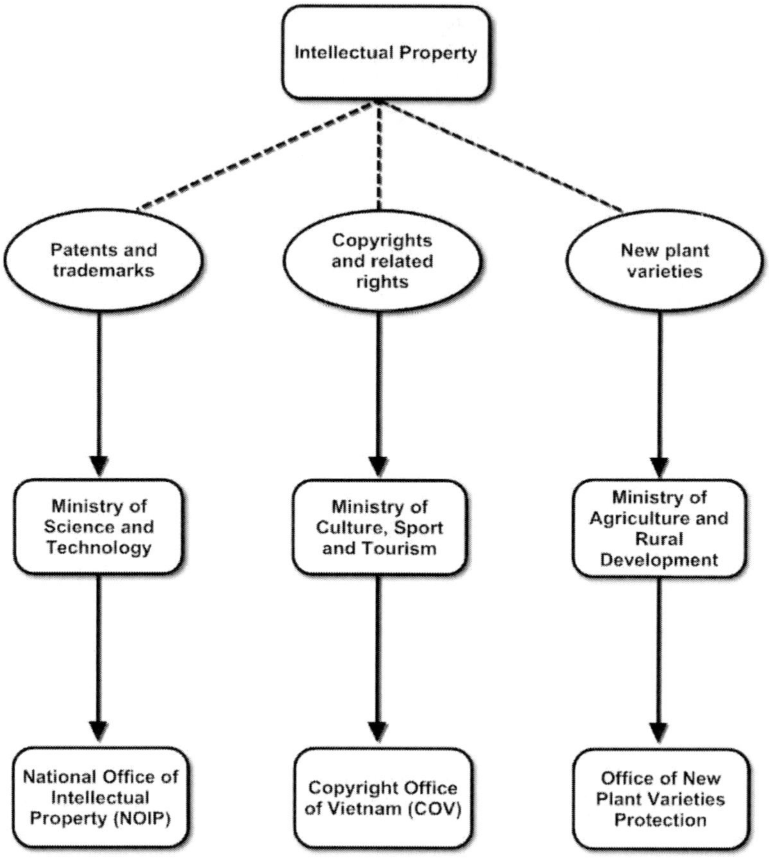

Source: Government of Vietnam, Inspectorate of Science and Technology, "Introduction to the IP Administration System of Vietnam," March 25, 2008.

Figure 6. IP administration in Vietnam is handled by several government agencies.

The Use of IPR in Vietnam Has Increased Substantially Since 2000

The number of patent and trademark applications submitted to Vietnam's NOIP increased by 189 percent during 2000–10. Patent applications totaled over 3,500 in 2010, with over 85 percent filed by foreigners (figure 7). The United States was the leading source of patent applications (832) followed closely by Japan (823) (figure 8). The large share of developed-country patent filings in part reflects the large pre-existing stock of patents in developed countries, as well as the generally low level of innovative capacity in Vietnam.[345] The small number of domestic patent applications is consistent with other developing countries that have low levels of research and development expenditures and few science and engineering graduates (see the "Education Services" section).[346] In addition, the patent application process is expensive and time consuming, and requires complex technical information; these costs may be more easily absorbed by large foreign companies.

The strong upward trend in trademark applications during the last decade reflects growth in Vietnam's business sector (figure 9). Trademark applications filed in Vietnam increased by nearly 400 percent during 2000–10, to nearly 28,000. Compared to patents, trademarks are easier and less costly to file, requiring less paperwork and technical documentation. Entities with a presence in the Vietnamese market accounted for over three-quarters of total applications filed in Vietnam in 2010. Many of these filers may be Vietnamese affiliates of foreign firms registering foreign trademarks, not indigenous Vietnamese companies, but available data do not distinguish between the two types.[347] However, an increasing number of indigenous Vietnamese trademark owners are reportedly being harmed by counterfeits, suggesting that some applications are from domestic businesses seeking protection.[348]

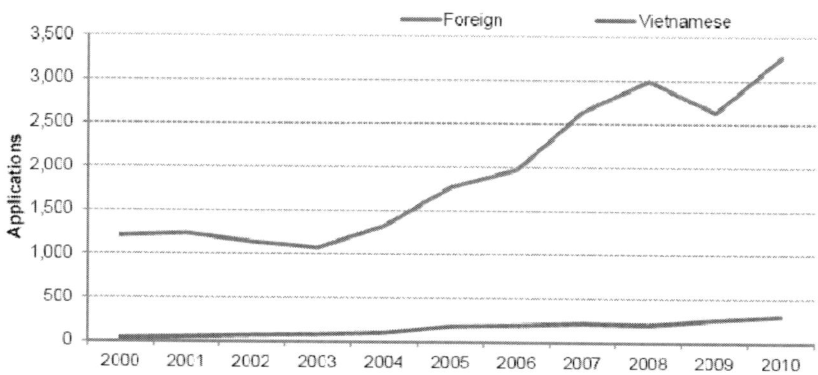

Source: Government of Vietnam, NOIP, "Intellectural Property Activities," 2010.

Figure 7. Patent applications by foreigners increased rapidly during 2000–2010.

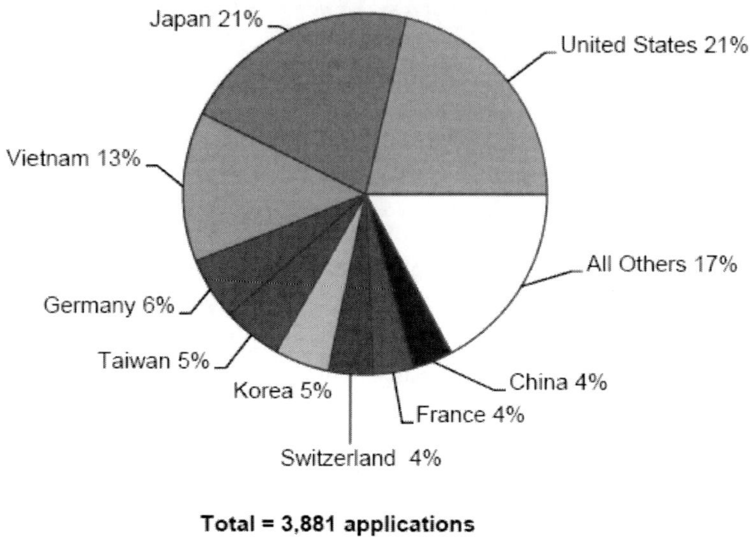

Source: Government of Vietnam, NOIP, "Intellectual Property Activities," April 2011.

Figure 8. U.S. and Japanese firms accounted for the largest share of patent applications in 2010.

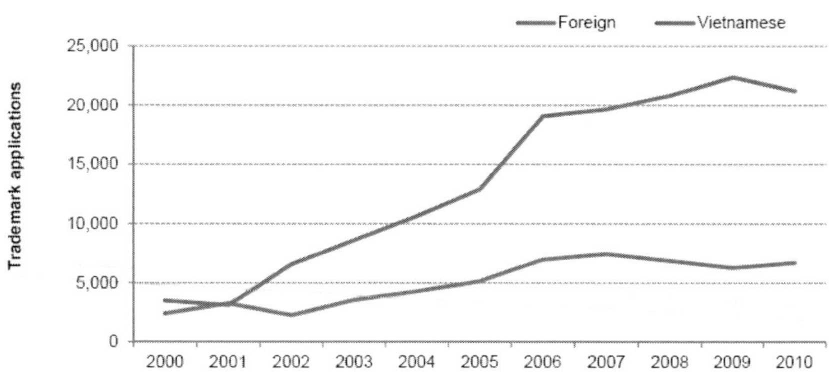

Source: Government of Vietnam, NOIP, "Intellectual Property Activities," April 2011.

Figure 9. Applications for trademarks increased substantially during 2000–10.

Despite Stronger IPR Laws, Infringement is Prevalent Due to Weak Enforcement

IPR infringement in Vietnam is reportedly widespread, posing a "significant market access barrier" to foreign firms in IP-intensive industries.[349] According to USTR, enforcement has not kept pace with the increase in infringement activities, and enforcement measures are not a significant deterrent to infringement.[350] Vietnam is designated as a "Watch List" country in USTR's 2011 Special 301 report, an annual review of IPR protection and enforcement. The report notes that there are high levels of copyright piracy in Vietnam, including increasing trade in online copyrighted files.[351] According to one source, 99 percent of the CD and DVD shops in major Vietnamese cities sell pirated goods.[352] Satellite and cable piracy is also common, and counterfeit goods (especially cosmetics, apparel, pharmaceuticals, and spirits) are reportedly ubiquitous in Vietnam's major cities.[353] Many of these products, along with other counterfeit products such as computers, software, watches, electronics, motorcycle parts, and food products, are smuggled in from China through Vietnam's northern border.[354]

Enforcement of IPR is usually handled administratively, which is reportedly straightforward and inexpensive compared to civil proceedings.[355] However, administrative remedies may fail to deter misbehavior, because remedial actions are infrequent and penalties are relatively small.[356] Moreover, administrative procedures are hampered by unclear areas of responsibility and a lack of coordination among enforcement agencies:[357] IP owners often do not know which agency to contact to address their IPR concerns.[358] Moreover, there is a shortage of trained personnel, technology, and other resources to process and oversee the rapidly increasing IP in Vietnam.[359]

Civil courts can provide preliminary injunctions and award damages, but filing court cases is relatively expensive and time consuming,[360] and IP owners are reluctant to spend time and money on civil cases when outcomes are uncertain.[361] Moreover, judges reportedly lack training in IP issues and there are few dedicated IP courts, which can add to the uncertainty of the civil court process.[362]

In theory, criminal prosecution can be brought by government authorities, with penalties including fines and jail terms.[363] However, as of the time of writing, no criminal infringement cases have been prosecuted in Vietnamese courts, in part because the implementing decrees and regulations regarding criminal laws have not yet been published.[364]

Vietnam Has Benefited from Both IPR Reforms and Infringement

There is a complex link between IPR and development, with both benefits and costs associated with strengthened IPR.[365] Economic theory suggests that countries that are climbing up the "technology ladder" have an incentive to improve IP protection in order to attract and create high technology and spur domestic innovation.[366] Conversely, countries at a lower stage of industrial growth with relatively weak innovative capacity have incentives to limit IPR in order to acquire and imitate technology inexpensively.[367] In terms of development, Vietnam may benefit both from a strengthened IPR framework and from relatively weak enforcement in certain areas of IP.

IPR reforms are generally associated with increased levels of trade, foreign direct investment (FDI), technology transfer, and innovation.[368] Since Vietnam instituted market and IPR reforms in preparation for its 2006 WTO accession, it has experienced substantial gains in most of these measures. Trade in services increased by 72 percent during 2005–08, reaching $15 billion before falling to $13 billion in 2009, and merchandise trade more than doubled to $143 billion in 2008 before declining in 2009.[369] Similarly, inbound FDI stocks increased from $31 billion in 2005 to $66 billion in 2010,[370] with a portion of this FDI in technology-intensive sectors such as communications, electronics, and chemicals, and in patent-intensive high-tech manufacturing and research and development.[371] An example of recent U.S. high-tech FDI in Vietnam includes Intel's $1 billion chip-testing facility, which opened in 2010.[372]

Vietnam's success in attracting FDI, however, may be based on factors other than strengthened IPR. Firms are interested in investing in Vietnam in order to access certain resources and competitive advantages.[373] For example, Intel may have been attracted by Vietnam's inexpensive labor, tax benefits, and proximity to China.[374] Moreover, for developing countries such as Vietnam, it is not clear whether strengthened IPR protections stimulate domestic innovation. There may be little impact for countries with limited technological capacity,[375] particularly when key complements to IPR, such as a quality education system, well-developed infrastructure, and a strong legal system, are lacking.[376]

For net importers of IP goods, such as Vietnam, there are some benefits associated with infringement. The use of pirated business software generates productivity gains for Vietnamese businesses, and consumer welfare rises from access to pirated sound and film recordings.[377] Moreover, producing and selling pirated and counterfeit goods can generate economic activity and employment.[378]

Vietnam's IPR regime is evolving. The Vietnamese public reportedly does not currently view infringement negatively, and sees little harm in using pirated products such as business software, CDs, and DVDs, or in purchasing counterfeit goods. However, the public is more sensitive to the dangers of counterfeit pharmaceuticals and food products, which can compromise health and safety.[379] Among domestic creators and owners of IP, there is a growing effort to reduce infringement. Vietnamese writers and musicians are forming organizations to advocate for increased protections and promote educational programs on copyright violations;[380] for example, Vietnamese music artists have established the Vietnam Center for Protection of Music Copyright to protect their artistic works.[381] Vietnamese trademark owners are also raising concerns as their goods and services are increasingly counterfeited. As Vietnam's economy continues to develop, there likely will be increased pressure from indigenous IP stakeholders to strengthen enforcement of IPR.

References

Branstetter, Lee, C. Fritz Foley, and Kamal Saggi. "Has the Shift to Stronger Intellectual Property Rights Promoted Technology Transfer, FDI, and Industrial Development?" *WIPO Journal* 2, issue 1 (2010). http://www.scribd.com/doc/87627742/Wipo-Journal-Volume-2-Issue-1-2010.

Cepeda, Ricardo H. Cavazos, Douglas C. Lippoldt, and Jonathan Senft. "Policy Complements to the Strengthening of IPRs in Developing Countries." Organisation for Economic Co-operation and Development (OECD). Working Party of the Trade Committee. Working paper 104, September 14, 2010. http://www.oecd.org/officialdocuments/display documentpdf?cote=TAD/TC/WP(2010)12/FINAL &doclanguage=en.

Commission on Intellectual Property Rights. "Integrating Intellectual Property Rights and Development Policy." London: Department for International Development, November 2002.

Economist Intelligence Unit (EIU). *Country Commerce: Vietnam*. New York: Economist Intelligence Unit, 2011.

Financial Times. FDI Markets Database. http://www.fdimarkets.com/ (accessed September 12, 2011). Global Software Alliance (GSA). *Eighth Annual BSA Global Software 2010 Piracy Study,* May 2011.

Government of Vietnam. Copyright Office of Vietnam. http://www.cov.gov.vn/English/home.asp (accessed June 1, 2011).

———. General Statistics Office (GSO). "Exports and Imports of Services" and "Export and Imports of Goods." http://www.gso.gov.vn/default en.aspx?tabid=472&idmid=3&ItemID=11814 (accessed June 1, 2011).

———. GSO. "Foreign Direct Investment Projects Licensed in 2009 by Main Counterparts." http://www.gso.gov.vn/default_en.aspx?tabid=491 (accessed June 12, 2011).

———. Inspectorate of Science and Technology. "Introduction to the IP Administration System of Vietnam," March 25, 2008. http://ipr enforcement.most.gov.vn/ckfinder/userfiles/files/Introduction%20to%20th e%20IP%20a dministration%20system%20of%20Vietnam % 282%29. pdf.

———. National Office of Intellectual Property (NOIP). "Intellectual Property Activities, 2010 Annual Report," April 2011. http://noip.gov.vn/noip/ resource.nsf/vwResourceList/53DB75F675B9E5CD47257895002F54BB/ $FILE/Annual%20report FINAL 05-2010.pdf.

INSEAD. "The Global Innovation Index 2011: Accelerating Growth and Development." 2011. http://www.globalinnovationindex.org/gii/main/ previous/ 2010-11/FullReport 10-11.pdf.

International Anticounterfeiting Coalition (IACC). Written submission to the United States Trade Representative in connection with the 2011 Special 301 report, February 15, 2011.

International Intellectual Property Alliance (IIPA).Written submission to the United States Trade Representative in connection with the 2010 Special 301 report, February 15, 2011.

Maskus, Keith E. *Intellectual Property Rights in the Global Economy*. Washington, DC: Institute for International Economics, 2000.

Motion Picture Association of America (MPAA). "Trade Barriers to Exports of U.S. Filmed Entertainment," November 2009. http://www.mpaa.org/ Resources/4bb10c1f-b0b2-4403-8b2af4ea519a0645.pdf.

Nystedt, Dan. "Intel Opens $1 Billion Chip Factory in Vietnam." *Computer World,* October 29, 2010. http://www.computerworld.com/ s/article/ 9193919/Intel opens 1 billion chip factory in Vietna m.

Park, W.G., and D. Lippoldt. "Technology Transfer and the Economic Implications of the Strengthening of Intellectual Property Rights in Developing Countries." Organisation for Economic Cooperation and Development (OECD). Trade Policy Working Paper Number 62. Paris: OECD, January 25, 2008.

Social Science Research Council (SRRC). *Media Piracy in Emerging Economies*, 2011. Hunter Rodwell Consulting. "Intellectual Property Rights Primer for Vietnam," June 2008.

United Nations, UNCTAD Stat. http://unctadstat.unctad.org/TableViewer/tableView.aspx (accessed September 12, 2011).

U.S. Department of Commerce (USDOC). U.S. Commercial Service (USCS). *Doing Business in Vietnam: 2011 Country Commercial Guide for U.S. Companies*, 2011.

U.S. International Trade Commission (USITC), *China: Intellectual Property Infringement, Indigenous Innovation Policies, and Frameworks for Measuring the Effects on the U.S. Economy*. USITC Publication 4199. Washington, DC: USITC, 2010.

———. Hearing transcript in connection with inv. no 332-514, *China: Intellectual Property Infringement, Indigenous Innovation Policies, and Frameworks for Measuring the Effects on the U.S. Economy*, June 15, 2010. https://edis.usitc.gov/edis3-internal/app (free registration required).

United States Trade Representative (USTR). "Vietnam." *2011 National Trade Estimate Report on Foreign Trade Barriers*. Washington, DC: USTR, 2011. http://www.ustr.gov/webfm_send/2748.

———. *Special 301 Report, 2011*. Washington DC, 2011.

U.S.-Vietnam Trade Council. "Summary of the Agreement between the U.S. and Vietnam on Trade Relations," May 10, 2004. http://www.usvtc.org/trade/bta/survey.pdf.

Vietnam Center for Protection of Music Copyright (VCPMC) [in Vietnamese]. http://vcpmc.org/vcpmc/content/36/gioi-thieu/ (accessed September 12, 2011).

World Intellectual Property Organization (WIPO). " What Is Intellectual Property?" http://www.wipo.int/about-ip/en/ (accessed September 12, 2011).

End Notes

[1] Vietnam Prime Minister, "Decision No. 175/QD-TTg," January 27, 2011.

[2] The Vietnamese population in the United States was an estimated 1.6 million in 2010; U.S. Census Bureau, "2010 American Community Survey," 2010.

[3] Previous working papers covered India and Malaysia; see http://www.usitc.gov/research_and_analysis/staff_products.htm.

[4] World Bank, WDI Online database (accessed February 15, 2012). The World Bank defines lower-middle-income countries as those with gross national income per capita between $1,000 and $4,000 in 2011.

[5] EIU, "Vietnam Economy, Politics and GDP Growth Summary," n.d. (accessed February 15, 2012).

[6] Government of Vietnam, General Statistics Office, *The Enterprises in Viet Nam*, 2010, 29.

[7] U.S. Department of State, *Background Notes: Vietnam*, November 30, 2010.

[8] Government of Vietnam, General Statistics Office, *The Enterprises in Viet Nam*, 2010, 30.

[9] ADB, "Viet Nam," December 2009, 39.

[10] Ibid., 37.

[11] U.S. Department of State, *Background Notes: Vietnam*, November 3, 2010.

[12] Government of Vietnam, Foreign Investment Agency, "Information about FDI," n.d. (accessed June 22, 2011). Total numbers for service FDI projects may be higher, as some categories of FDI were not clearly labeled.

[13] Ibid.

[14] EIU analyst, e-mail message to USITC staff, February 22, 2011.

[15] World Economic Forum, "Global Competitiveness Report 2011-2012," 2011, 368. Other barriers include inadequate access to financing, policy instability, and foreign currency regulations.

[16] U.S. Commercial Service official, e-mail message to USITC staff, February 14, 2011.

[17] Transparency International, "Corruption Perception Index 2011," 2011. A lower score represents less corruption.

[18] Global Integrity Report, "Vietnam: 2009." A higher score represents less corruption.

[19] Only 30 percent of Vietnamese judges have a law degree; many judges obtain their posts through political connections, making them hesitant to challenge government actions.

[20] The World Bank, along with the Vietnamese government and other bilateral donors, has organized an anti-corruption initiative program. At the time of writing, the project was screening proposals.

[21] World Bank, "Doing Business 2012," 2012, 76. A lower score represents a better business environment.

[22] Mackey, "Vietnam Seeks Billions for Ports Overhaul," December 9, 2009.

[23] EIU analyst, e-mail correspondence with USITC staff, February 22, 2011.

[24] Euromonitor International, "Country Factfile."

[25] ITU, "Vietnam Ends December with 170 Mln Telephony Subs," January 13, 2011.

[26] Government of Vietnam, General Statistics Office, *Enterprises' Data of the Year 2000–2008*, 2009, 3.

[27] VietnamNet, "E-Commerce Set to Boom in 2010," February 16, 2010.

[28] CIA World Fact Book, "Economy Overview."

[29] General Statistics Office of Vietnam, *The Enterprises in Viet Nam*, 2010, 28.

[30] Vietnam Prime Minister, "Decision No. 175/QD-TTg," January 27, 2011.

[31] The 10 members of ASEAN are Brunei, Burma, Cambodia, Indonesia, Laos, Malaysia, the Philippines, Singapore, Thailand, and Vietnam.

[32] World Bank, "WDI Online Database."

[33] EIU, "Thailand Economy, Politics and GDP Growth Summary," n.d. (accessed February 15, 2012).

[34] EIU, "Philippines Economy, Politics and GDP Growth Summary," n.d. (accessed February 15, 2012).

[35] EIU, "Indonesia Economy, Politics and GDP Growth Summary," n.d. (accessed February 15, 2012).

[36] EIU, *Long-Term Outlook: Vietnam*, 2011.

[37] EIU, *Long-Term Outlook: Thailand*, 2011.

[38] EIU, *Long-Term Outlook: Singapore*, 2011.

[39] EIU, *Long-Term Outlook: Philippines*, 2011.

[40] Vietnam's exports and imports each accounted for less than 1 percent of the world total in 2010. WTO, *International Trade Statistics 2011*, 2011, 184–94, tables A8 and A9.

[41] Calculations based on WTO, *International Trade Statistics 2011*, 2011, 184–94, tables A8 and A9.

[42] Cany, "Vietnam Business Forum," December 2, 2010.

[43] Transportation services refer to the transport of passengers or freight by road, rail, sea, or air. Freight transportation services are generally associated with manufacturing trade, while passenger transportation services, in tandem with travel services, contribute to the development of tourism (both business and leisure).

[44] The tourism sector includes services provided by a number of industries, including the (passenger) transportation, travel, hotel, and restaurant industries.

[45] Other categories include business travelers. Government of Vietnam, VNAT, "International Visitors to Vietnam in December and 12 Months of 2009," January 10, 2010; Government of Vietnam, VNAT, "International Visitors to Vietnam in December and 12 Months of 2010," January 6, 2011; Government of Vietnam, General Statistics Office, "Number of Foreign Visitors to Vietnam, 1996–pre-2009," n.d. (accessed November 16, 2011).

[46] The seven sites, in chronological order of inscription, are the complex of Hue monuments (1993); Ha Long Bay (1994); Hoi An Ancient Town (1999); My Son Sanctuary (1999); Phong Nha-Ke Bang National Park (2003); Central Sector of the Imperial Citadel of Thang Long–Hanoi (2010); and the Citadel of the Ho Dynasty (2011). UNESCO Web site, http://whc.unesco.org/en/statesparties/vn (accessed November 16, 2011).

[47] From 2008 to 2010, the number of Chinese visitors grew from 650,000 to 905,000, and in the first six months of 2011, Vietnam had already hosted 662,000 visitors from China. Government of Vietnam, VNAT, "International Visitors to Vietnam in December and 12 Months of 2008," December 30, 2008; "International Visitors to Vietnam in December and 12 Months of 2010," January 6, 2011; and "International Visitors to Vietnam in June and 6 Months of 2011," June 30, 2011.

[48] In 2008, the tourism industry was estimated to support 4.3 billion jobs and contribute $10.1 billion to GDP, up from $2.6 billion in 1999. World Travel and Tourism Council, Economic Data Search Tool, n.d. (accessed July 13, 2011).

[49] Government of Vietnam, VNAT, "Vietnam Okays Pact on More Flights to Australia," July 5, 2011.

[50] Singapore, Malaysia, Cambodia, Hong Kong, and China are among the most popular destinations for Vietnamese travelers. VNEconomynews.com, "Outbound Tourists Double in Number This Year," December 23, 2010.

[51] Ibid.

[52] As noted, transportation services, which move goods across borders, account for the second-largest share of Vietnam's external trade, following tourism. Hoekman and Mattoo, "Services Trade and Growth," December 2007, 3.

[53] Vietnam's Ministry of Planning and Investment, Central Institute of Economic Management and Foreign Investment Agency, and USAID-funded Support for Trade Acceleration

Project, "Assessment of the Five-Year Impact of the U.S.-Vietnam Bilateral Trade Agreement," July 2007, 2.

[54] EIU, "Vietnam," April 2011, 20, 74.

[55] Lobet, "Protecting Minority Shareholders to Boost Investment," 2008, 62. For example, the Laws on Investment and Enterprises, which went into effect July 1, 2006, attempted to unify Vietnam's foreign and domestic investment policies and establish a corporate-law regime for foreign and domestic enterprises. See Freshfields Bruckhaus Deringer, "Vietnam—New Investment Law," March 2006.

[56] There is a dearth of data on Vietnam's bilateral services trade, but among those countries that report services trade with Vietnam, Korea accounted for the largest single-country share of both imports and exports of services. At the time of writing Vietnam did not report bilateral trade data or trade volumes with its major services trading partners. Instead, data on Vietnam's imports and exports of services reflect trade volumes reported by partner countries. For example, Korea reported importing $1.58 billion of services from Vietnam in 2009 (corresponding to $1.58 billion of services exports from Vietnam to Korea). See OECD, OECD.Stat database.

[57] Calculations based on data from OECD, OECD.Stat database.

[58] Tran, "Vietnam and Korea Trade and Investment Ties Will Grow Strongly," September 9, 2010.

[59] Kien et al., "Dynamic Patterns of Korea-Vietnam Trade Relations," Summer 2010, 258.

[60] Cany, "Vietnam Business Forum," December 2, 2010, 1.

[61] Lee et al., "Vietnam: Selected Issues," December 2007, 15.

[62] Tran, "Vietnam and Korea Trade and Investment Ties Will Grow Strongly," September 9, 2010.

[63] Nhi, "Service Sector's Sloping Playing Field," November 5, 2010.

[64] Interview by USITC staff, Hanoi, December 6, 2010; Saich et al., "Choosing Success," January 2008, 31.

[65] Sectors related to national security, monopoly industries, and public welfare (such as industries involved in national defense, operation of flights and national transportation, and tobacco) remain fully state controlled. Majority state ownership is retained in 26 specific service sectors, including electricity production, finance, insurance, publishing, and telecommunications. Indochine Counsel, "Client Alert," February 2011; Government of Australia, Department of Foreign Affairs and Trade, "Vietnam Country Brief," March 2011.

[66] EIU, "Vietnam," April 2011, 10–12.

[67] There are no official data on the number of SOEs in place. U.S. Department of State, Bureau of Economic, Energy and Business Affairs, "2011 Investment Climate Statement," March 2011.

[68] Bureaucratic red tape and a lack of transparency are frequently cited as barriers to doing business in Vietnam. Industry representatives, interview by USITC staff, Hanoi, December 8, 2010; Hui et al., "Vietnam," 2010, 3.

[69] Only 5 percent of Vietnam's visitors return for a second visit, while Thailand's return rate is 50 percent. *Economist*, "Laying a Thousand-year Egg," October 8, 2010.

[70] Unlike Malaysia and Thailand, which offer tourist visa exemptions to citizens of many countries, including the United States and Europe, Vietnam requires a visa of all visitors except those from ASEAN nations. Eurocham, "Position Paper: Tourism and Hospitality," 2011, 2.

[71] *TBKTVN*, "Complicated Procedures Hinder Vietnam's Tourism Development," January 6, 2011.

[72] Bland, "Vietnam Tourism," June 6, 2011.

[73] *Economist*, "Laying a Thousand-year Egg," October 8, 2010.

[74] Ibid.

[75] Government of Vietnam, Vietnam Ministry of Foreign Affairs, "General Information about Countries and Regions," April 26, 2011.

[76] Cany, "Vietnam Business Forum," December 2, 2010; Government of Vietnam, "Resolution on Simplifying 258 Administrative Procedures," June 2, 2006.

[77] APEC's 21 members are largely made up of the Pacific Rim countries and include Australia, Canada, Chile, China, Japan, and the United States.

[78] The ASEAN-Korea agreement on trade in services was signed in 2007; an agreement with India covering trade in goods was signed in 2009, as well as a deal with Australia and New Zealand to create a trans-Pacific free trade zone; and an FTA with China took effect on January 1, 2010. EIU, "Vietnam," April 2011, 20.

[79] Vietnam's Ministry of Planning and Investment, Central Institute of Economic Management and Foreign Investment Agency, and USAID-funded Support for Trade Acceleration Project, "Assessment of the Five-Year Impact of the U.S.-Vietnam Bilateral Trade Agreement," July 2007, 2; Lobet, "Protecting Minority Shareholders to Boost Investment," 2008, 62.

[80] Ibid, 5. Goods and services trade are often complementary; for example, the export of goods usually requires transportation and insurance services.

[81] EU countries reported exporting $1.6 billion in services to Vietnam in 2009, up from $687.7 million in 2006. Imports also rose, as EU countries imported $1.6 billion of services in 2009, compared to $1.1 billion in 2006. OECD, OECD.stat Database.

[82] EIU, "Vietnam," April 2011, 21; Patrikainen, "Vietnam, Chile Conclude Successful FTA Negotiations," June 23, 2011.

[83] The countries are Australia, Brunei, Chile, Japan, Malaysia, New Zealand, Peru, Singapore, the United States, and Vietnam.

[84] In October 2009, the two countries agreed to enter a strategic partnership, as well as initiate a feasibility study for a bilateral FTA. Tran, "Vietnam and Korea Trade and Investment Ties," September 9, 2010; Kiean, Lee, and Heo, "Dynamic Patterns of Korea-Vietnam Trade Relations," 2010, 258; EIU, "Vietnam," April 2011, 21.

[85] Business Advantage Vietnam, "Reforms Open Up Banking Sector," 2010, 14.

[86] Commercial banks are financial institutions that accept deposits and use them to provide loans or invest in capital markets, thereby transferring money from savers to borrowers. This intermediation function increases the efficiency of economic activity, and a well-functioning banking sector is a necessary part of the infrastructure of modern economies. Commercial banking services can be divided into two types: retail and wholesale. Retail banking services are purchased directly by individual consumers, while wholesale banking services are used by institutional clients such as corporations or pension funds.

[87] Federal Reserve Bank of San Francisco, *Asia Focus*, June 2011.

[88] Business Advantage Vietnam, "Reforms Open Up Banking Sector," 2010, 15.

[89] World Bank, World Development Indicators database.

[90] IMF, International Financial Statistics database.

[91] Federal Reserve Bank of San Francisco, *Asia Focus*, June 2011.

[92] Tran, "Analysis of the Vietnamese Banking Sector," 2008, 68.

[93] Pham and Lensink, "Lending Policies of Informal, Formal and Semiformal Lenders," 2007, 186.

[94] Ibid., 188.

[95] Maomi, "Current Situation on Consumer Credit in Vietnam," 2011, 6.
[96] Ibid., 2.
[97] Andrade et al., "How Young Consumers Could Shape Vietnam's Banks," March 2008.
[98] Maomi, "Current Situation on Consumer Credit in Vietnam," 2011, 6.
[99] Leung, "Banking and Financial Sector Reforms in Vietnam," 2009, 47.
[100] Reuters, "Vietnam Banks' Bad Debt Ratio Rises to 3.21 Pct in August," October 19, 2011.
[101] Reuters, "S&P: Vietnam Banks' SOE Loans May Harm Creditworthiness," December 12, 2010.
[102] Pham and Lensink, "Lending Policies of Informal, Formal and Semiformal Lenders," 2007, 193.
[103] Fitch Ratings, "2011 Outlook," January 31, 2011.
[104] Ibid.
[105] Tran, "Analysis of the Vietnamese Banking Sector," 2008, 76.
[106] Nguyen et al., "Trust and Uncertainty," 2006, 557.
[107] One manager of a private bank explained, "How to get the market price is not an easy task. The real estate offices and companies can be one reference. Sometimes they do not cooperate, because we do not buy their goods and services. We have to go to the neighborhood, look at the newspaper, consult real state offices, etc., and still feel insecure about our estimates." Ibid., 556.
[108] Ibid., 557.
[109] Ibid., 559.
[110] The four original SOCBs include Bank for Agriculture and Rural Development (Agribank), Bank for Investment and Development (BIDV), Bank for Foreign Trade (Vietcombank), and Industrial and Commercial Bank (Vietinbank). Eventually the Vietnamese government created the Mekong Housing Bank (MHB) and the Vietnam Bank for Social Policies to help serve the needs of the poor.
[111] Kovsted et al., "From Monobank to Commercial Banking," 2006, 103.
[112] Foreign banks operating in Vietnam are subject to minimum capital requirements and other commonly encountered regulations.
[113] Federal Reserve Bank of San Francisco, *Asia Focus*, June 2011.
[114] *Vietnam Business News*, "Banks Raise Chartered Capital by 600 Times in 9 Years," June 15, 2010.
[115] Standard & Poor's, "Industry Report Card," July 24, 2011.
[116] Chan, "New State Bank of Vietnam Guidelines Lack Clarity," June 2011.
[117] EU-Vietnam MUTRAP, "Comprehensive Strategy for Service Sector Development," December 2009, 292.
[118] Ibid., 292.
[119] Federal Reserve Bank of San Francisco, *Asia Focus*, June 2011.
[120] Leung, "Banking and Financial Sector Reforms in Vietnam," 2009, 48.
[121] These banks include HSBC (UK), Standard Chartered Bank (UK), ANZ Bank (Australia), Shinhan Bank (Korea), and Hong Leong Bank (Malaysia).
[122] Reuters, "Vietnam Banks' Bad Debt Ratio Rises to 3.21 Pct in August," October 19, 2011.
[123] McNulty, "In-house Wary over Banks' Vietnam Investment," September 2011.
[124] Waal et al., "High Performance in Vietnam," 2009, 193.
[125] Federal Reserve Bank of San Francisco, *Asia Focus*, June 2011.
[126] Standard & Poor's, "Industry Report Card," July 24, 2011.
[127] Overland, "As Vietnam Expands Its Higher-Education System," July 1, 2008.
[128] Asian Development Bank, "Viet Nam," August 2010, 6.

[129] Overland, "American Colleges Raise the Flag in Vietnam," May 15, 2009.

[130] Vietnam Business Forum, *Position Paper*, December 2007, 1.

[131] USDOC, U.S. Commercial Service, "Vietnam's Market for Education and Training," March 2010.

[132] Institute of International Education, "International Student Enrollments Rose Modestly in 2009/10," November 15, 2010. The leading countries sending students to the United States that year, by rank, were China, India, Korea, Canada, Taiwan, Japan, Saudi Arabia, and Mexico.

[133] EIU, *Country Report: Vietnam*, June 2011, 8.

[134] Institute of International Education, "International Student Enrollments Rose Modestly in 2009/10," November 15, 2010; USDOC, U.S. Commercial Service, "Vietnam's Market for Education and Training," March 2010.

[135] USDOC, U.S. Commercial Service, "Vietnam's Market for Education and Training," March 2010 and Int-Hout, "Vietnamese Students Overcome Hurdles to Study in America," February 16, 2011.

[136] Vallely and Wilkinson, "Vietnamese Higher Education," November 2008, 2; Ca, "Universities as Drivers of the Urban Economies in Asia," June 2006, 4.

[137] Library of Congress, "Education," 1989. Under Confucianism, education was essential for admission to the ruling class of scholar-officials, the mandarinate.

[138] Trung and Swierczek, "Skills Development in Higher Education in Vietnam," October 2009, 579; Ca, "Universities as Drivers of the Urban Economies in Asia," June 2006, 11–13.

[139] Vallely and Wilkinson, "Vietnamese Higher Education," November 2008, 2.

[140] Trung and Swierczek, "Skills development in higher education in Vietnam," October 2009, 565–6.

[141] Ibid., 565–7.

[142] Ibid., 579.

[143] Vietnam Business Forum, *Position Paper*, December 2007, 1-2.

[144] Vallely and Wilkinson, "Vietnamese Higher Education," November 2008, 2.

[145] Vietnam Business Forum, *Position Paper*, December 2007, 2-4, and Social Republic of Vietnam, Ministry of Education and Training, "Report," October 29, 2009, 17-19.

[146] Saich et al., "Choosing Success," January 2008, 3–5.

[147] Vietnam Business Forum, *Position Paper*, December 2007, 2–4; industry officials, interviews by USITC staff, Hanoi, Vietnam, December 6–10, 2010.

[148] Ca, "Universities as Drivers of the Urban Economies in Asia," June 2006, 11–14; Vallely and Wilkinson, "Vietnamese Higher Education," November 2008, 2-3. The problems Vietnam faces in higher education are, in part, a consequence of its history. The French colonial regime that ruled Vietnam until 1945 invested very little in higher education (compared to other regional colonial powers). As a result, Vietnam missed the boom in institutional investment and growth that swept through most of the region in the early 20th century, when many of Asia's leading universities were founded. After independence, Vietnam's weak tertiary education system was put under the control of the government, whose cumbersome decision-making processes make changes difficult to implement.

[149] Runckel, "The Education System in Vietnam," 2009; Di Gropello, "Vietnam: Higher Education and Skills for Growth," 2007; OECD, *Education at a Glance, 2011*, 398. By comparison, student-faculty ratios in Malaysia are about 20:1 and about 15:1 in Indonesia. OECD countries such as Iceland, Japan, Norway, and Sweden have student-faculty ratios closer to about 11:1.

[150] Vietnam Trade Office in the United States, "Business Environment," April 22, 2008.

[151] Overland, "As Vietnam Expands Its Higher-Education System," July 1, 2008.
[152] Wasley, "Vietnamese Leaders, on U.S. Visit, Discuss Ambitious Overhaul," July 21, 2007.
[153] Overland, "As Vietnam Expands Its Higher-Education System," July 1, 2008.
[154] Vallely and Wilkinson, "Vietnamese Higher Education," November 2008, 2–3. See the "Intellectual Property Rights" section.
[155] Business-in-Asia.com, "The Education System in Vietnam," 2009.
[156] Trung and Swierczek, "Skills Development in Higher Education in Vietnam," October 2009, 565–67.
[157] Ca, "Universities as Drivers of the Urban Economies in Asia," June 2006, 11–14.
[158] Vallely and Wilkinson, "Vietnamese Higher Education," November 2008, 2–3.
[159] Overland, "American Colleges Raise the Flag in Vietnam," May 15, 2009; Vallely and Wilkinson, "Vietnamese Higher Education," November 2008, 2–3.
[160] Overland, "American Colleges Raise the Flag in Vietnam," May 15, 2009.
[161] Ibid.
[162] Ibid. However, reportedly much of the appeal of Troy's Vietnam program is that it caters to those who fail to get into a Vietnamese university. Vietnam remains a relatively low-income nation, and only the small upper middle class can afford to send their children to the more expensive joint degree programs or abroad. Most Vietnamese university and college students struggle to cover the $130 average annual tuition that their local public institutions generally charge, and programs such as those offered by Troy University, despite their high reputation, are a second choice for many students.
[163] Industry officials, interviews by USITC staff, Hanoi, Vietnam, December 6–10, 2010.
[164] Overland, "American Colleges Raise the Flag in Vietnam," May 15, 2009.
[165] Ibid.
[166] *Chronicle of Higher Education*, "Private Universities in Vietnam Draw Fire," April 13, 2010.
[167] USITC, *Logistic Services*, May 2005, 1-2 and 1-3. Logistics firms may transport services as well—for example, in the form of building plans prepared by architectural services firms or legal briefs prepared by law firms.
[168] Armstrong & Associates, Inc., "U.S. 3PL Market Size Estimates," 2009.
[169] OECD, "Transport Logistics," 2002, 14–15.
[170] Transport Intelligence, *Vietnam Logistics 2009*, February 2009, 6; *Viet NamNet Bridge*, "Vietnam Works to Gain Market Share in Logistics Services," September 11, 2007; Johnson, "Vietnam on the Verge," *American Shipper*, December 2007. The majority of Vietnamese logistics firms have been characterized as "mom-and-pop" ventures with five employees or less and no more than $30,000 in annual revenues.
[171] Transport Intelligence, *Vietnam Logistics 2009*, February 2009, 45.
[172] Armstrong & Associates, Inc., "Global 3PL & Logistics Outsourcing Strategy," 2011.
[173] This amount pertains to 3PL revenues only, which represent only a portion of Vietnam's total logistics costs.
[174] Transport Intelligence, *Vietnam Logistics 2009*, February 2009, 47–48.
[175] ILO, *Vietnam Employment Trends*, 2010, 13. The modest size of the increase in employment forecasted for Vietnam's logistics sector may be due, in part, to a potential rise in the sector's labor productivity.
[176] CIO, "Vietnam—Road Development Brief," January 8, 2010; CIO, "Vietnam—Port Development Brief," December 3, 2009; CIO, "Vietnam—Air Transport and Infrastructure," September 23, 2010; Government of Vietnam, MPT, "Services Sector Development," November 2005, 13.
[177] *Business Advantage Vietnam*, "Logistics Providers Make New Investments," 2010, 25.

[178] CIO, "Vietnam—The Increasing Presence of DHL in Vietnam," November 19, 2009; Transport Intelligence, *Vietnam Logistics 2009*, February 2009, 56–61.

[179] Government of Vietnam, MPT, "Vietnam's IPs, EPZs and EZs," June 2007, 23; Transport Intelligence, *Vietnam Logistics 2009*, February 2009, 37, 40.

[180] Transport Intelligence, *Vietnam Logistics 2009*, February 2009, 18.

[181] Government of Vietnam, General Statistics Office, "Volume of Freight by Type of Transport," n.d., and "Volume of Freight by Transport Sector," n.d. (accessed March 15, 2011).

[182] CIO, "Vietnam—Port Development Brief," December 3, 2009.

[183] APL and Frost & Sullivan, "Vietnam Transportation and Logistics," 2007, 5.

[184] *Business Advantage Vietnam,* "Driven to Expansion," 2010, 23; Hutchison Port Holdings, "Saigon International Terminals Vietnam"; *Supply Chain Management*, "Vietnam," September 25, 2008. Roughly 60 to 70 percent of imports and exports in Vietnam are reportedly shipped through Ho Chi Minh City.

[185] Bloomberg, "Maersk APM Terminals to Develop Container Terminal in Vietnam," July 21, 2008.

[186] APM Terminals, "Deepwater Access Deemed Key to Vietnam Port Utilization," October 14, 2010.

[187] Transport Intelligence, *Vietnam Logistics 2009*, February 2009, 27.

[188] Ibid., 25; CIO, "Vietnam—Air Transport and Infrastructure," September 23, 2010.

[189] Transport Intelligence, *Vietnam Logistics 2009*, February 2009, 25; Putzger, "Bullish Integrators Step Up Asia Flights," June 7, 2010; FedEx, "New FedEx Flight from Hanoi Improves Transit Time," November 18, 2010.

[190] Vietnam is working to liberalize its air transport services market under bilateral and multilateral agreements; see below.

[191] Transport Intelligence, *Vietnam Logistics 2009*, February 2009, 36. The rail system in Vietnam is run by a state-owned entity, Vietnam Railways Corporation.

[192] Transport Intelligence, *Vietnam Logistics 2009*, February 2009, 40–41.

[193] Johnson, "Vietnam on the Verge," December 2007. It reportedly takes an average of 29 hours to travel south by rail from Hanoi to Ho Chi Minh City, a distance of about 700 miles.

[194] Transport Intelligence, *Vietnam Logistics 2009*, February 2009, 40–41, Government of Vietnam, General Statistics Office, "Volume of Freight by Type of Transport," n.d. (accessed March 17, 2011). The remaining freight is transported by water and air.

[195] *Vietnam Business and Economy News*, "A Fresh Start for Infrastructure Investment," January 17, 2011. On January 15, 2011, the Vietnamese government passed legislation to encourage private sector participation in new infrastructure projects including airports, seaports, railways, bridges, tunnels, power plants, wastewater treatment plants, and hospitals. Projects approved by the government must be funded with 70 percent private funds and 30 percent Vietnamese state funds. Investors in PPPs are offered incentives for their involvement, such as corporate tax breaks and exemptions from land use fees. Goods imported or exported in connection with projects are also eligible for tax preferences.

[196] GEA, "Vietnam," November 20, 2009.

[197] World Bank, *Doing Business 2011*, 2011, 56–57. The composite index ranks countries by their customs environments using three criteria: the number of documents it takes to import to and export from a country, the time it takes to import and export, and the costs associated with import and export. Each factor is given a weight of one-third.

[198] Ibid., 53–59. The time it takes to export and import goods from a particular country is calculated based on the time used for obtaining necessary export and import documents,

inland transport and handling, customs clearance and inspections, and port and terminal handling. By comparison with Vietnam, it takes about 14 days to export and import goods from the Philippines and Thailand, up to 20 days to export goods to Indonesia, and 48 days to export goods to Laos. (Importing goods from Indonesia and Laos is relatively more efficient than exporting to these countries, as imports take an estimated 6 and 10 days, respectively.)

[199] Transport Intelligence, *Vietnam Logistics 2009*, February 2009, 45.

[200] Ibid., 45; Lee, "Multinationals Take a Longer View of Vietnam," April 11, 2009.

[201] Government of Vietnam, MPT, "Vietnam's IPs, EPZs and EZs," June 2007, 5.

[202] UNCTAD, *Investment Policy Review*, 2008, 11.

[203] *Vietnam Business News*, "High-Tech Multinationals Invest in VN," September 28, 2010; *Vietnam Business News*, "TNT Vietnam Expands Logistics Capacity," January 23, 2010; and UNCTAD, *Investment Policy* Review, 2008, 18.

[204] DHL, "DHL Invests Ahead of the Curve," June 23, 2009.

[205] Kuehne + Nagel, "Heavy Lift Express in Vietnam," n.d. (accessed March 24, 2011).

[206] Transport Intelligence, *Vietnam Logistics 2009*, February 2009, 58–65; Panalpina, "Annual Report 2009," 2009, 31; *Global News*, "Nippon Express Augments Logistics Services in Vietnam," March 16, 2010.

[207] Transport Intelligence, *Vietnam Logistics 2009*, February 2009, 58.

[208] DHL, "DHL Invests Ahead of the Curve," June 23, 2009.

[209] Panalpina, "Annual Report 2009," 2009, 31.

[210] D.B. Schenker, "Schenker Vietnam." Schenker opened the logistics center in conjunction with its joint venture partner, Vietnamese maritime shipping firm Gemadept.

[211] Panalpina, "Annual Report 2009," 2009, 31.

[212] Transport Intelligence, *Vietnam Logistics 2009*, February 2009, 60–61; and Cuchi Shipping Company, "Introduction."

[213] Putzger, "Bullish Integrators Step Up Asia Flights," June 7, 2010.

[214] UN, Statistics Division, United Nations Service Trade database, 2010.

[215] USITC staff calculations based on data from WTO, "World Trade in Transportation Services by Region, 2008," and WTO, "Leading Exporters and Importers of Transportation Services, 2008."

[216] USITC staff calculations based on data from UN Statistics Division, United Nations Service Trade database, 2010, and WTO, "World Trade in Transportation Services by Region, 2008."

[217] WTO, Statistical Division, "Country Profiles: Vietnam," October 2010. In 2009, the top three categories of Vietnamese exports and imports were manufactures, agricultural goods, and fuels and mining products. In general, lightweight, high-value goods (as well as perishables) tend to be transported by air, whereas heavier goods, such as machinery and transportation equipment, are often transported by ship.

[218] Johnson, "Vietnam on the Verge," December 2007. The United States accounts for approximately 40 percent of the volume of Vietnam's air freight exports. Textiles, footwear, and seafood are among the largest categories of goods transported by air from Vietnam, while electronic products represent an increasing share of these exports.

[219] U.N. Comtrade, "Viet Nam," n.d. (accessed March 23, 2011).

[220] Johnson, "Vietnam on the Verge," December 2007.

[221] WTO, "Working Party on the Accession of Viet Nam," October 27, 2006.

[222] The GATS excludes commitments on air passenger and air freight transportation services.

[223] WTO, "Working Party on the Accession of Viet Nam," October 27, 2006, 45–51.

[224] ASEAN, "ASEAN Framework Agreement for the Integration of Priority Sectors;" Vietnam Business Forum, "Logistics Integration," September 7, 2010; UN Economic Commission for Europe, "The Single Window Concept," April 2003. A single customs window permits exporters and importers to submit all documentation related to the release and clearance of goods to a single, rather than multiple, government agencies.

[225] Vietnam Business Forum, "Logistics Integration," September 7, 2010.

[226] ADB, "Connecting Greater Mekong Subregion Railways," August 2010, 7; Transport Intelligence, *Vietnam Logistics 2009*, February 2009, 17. The Greater Mekong Subregion (GMS) includes Burma / Myanmar, Cambodia, China, Laos, Thailand, and Vietnam. In addition to transportation, the GMS infrastructure plan includes improving regional connectivity in telecommunications and electric power, and strengthening network linkages between the GMS and neighboring Asian countries.

[227] ASEAN, "ASEAN Multilateral Agreement on the Full Liberalisation," May 20, 2009.

[228] Binh, "CAAV Says Will Open Skies for Qualified Foreign Airlines," November 13, 2008.

[229] Vietnam Business Forum, "Logistics Integration," September 7, 2010.

[230] *Viet NamNet Bridge*, "What's the Aviation Market in the WTO?" December 21, 2006; InterVISTAS-EU Consulting, "The Impact of International Air Service Liberalisation," July 2009, iii.

[231] FedEx, "New FedEx Flight from Vietnam Improves Transit Time," November 18, 2010.

[232] U.S. Census Bureau, "2007 NAICS Definition," 2007.

[233] Government of Vietnam, General Statistics Office, "Structure of Employed Population," n.d. (accessed April 7, 2011); Government of Vietnam, General Statistics Office, "Structure of Gross Domestic Product," n.d. (accessed April 13, 2011). The employment figures quoted here refer to the employed population above 15 years of age. The figures for 2009 are preliminary.

[234] *Đổi mới* ("renovation") was the name given by Vietnam's government to the series of reforms intended to move the economy from central planning to a "socialist-oriented market economy."

[235] Figuié and Moustier, "Market Appeal in an Emerging Economy," April 2009, 210; Maruyama and Trung, "Modern Retailers in Transition Economies," March 10, 2011, 3.

[236] Maruyama and Trung, "Modern Retailers in Transition Economies," March 10, 2011, 8–9.

[237] A number of observers have sought to characterize generalized patterns of evolution of the modern retail industry in developing countries. Wrigley and Lowe (2010) review this literature. According to Reardon et al. (2003), supermarkets first establish a foothold in capital cities as niche shopping destinations for the wealthy, then become more important to poorer consumers there as the supermarkets build economies of scale and prices decline. They then spread to smaller cities and towns and rural areas. Reviewing work by Reardon et al. and others, Figuié and Moustier (2009) describe a process whereby supermarkets take an increasing share of the market from traditional retailers and the number of retail outlets shrinks overall. However, as noted by Wrigley and Lowe, others have argued that this model is overly deterministic and that traditional markets are often able to hold their own against competition from supermarkets, especially for retail of fresh food.

[238] Planet Retail Database (accessed April 12, 2011). These figures are in current dollars. The increase was not as dramatic in real terms because consumer prices increased by 55.4 percent over the same period (IMF, World Economic Outlook Database, April 2011).

[239] Planet Retail database (accessed April 12, 2011).

[240] Company representative, quoted in McKinsey & Company, "Understanding the New Vietnam," June 2010; Breu, Salsberg, and Tú, "Growing Up Fast," August 2010, 3.

[241] Breu, Salsberg, and Tú, "Growing Up Fast," August 2010, 4.

[242] Planet Retail, "Country Report: Vietnam," April 6, 2011, 21. Bargaining ("haggling") is common in traditional markets in Vietnam and many other developing countries. Bargaining enables sellers to extract greater margins from those customers willing to pay the most, and enables buyers to purchase goods at prices that more finely reflect their willingness to pay. However, bargaining takes time—a cost for the buyer and seller alike. Fixed prices thus appeal to both buyers and sellers as their earning power—and the opportunity cost of their time—increases. Fixed prices also become more common as chain stores take an increasing share of a retail market, as such prices enable a chain's leaders to exert control over margins despite having dispersed points of sale. Cason, Friedman, and Milam, "Bargaining versus Posted Price Competition," February 2003, 225.

[243] Maruyama and Trung, "Modern Retailers in Transition Economies," March 10, 2011, 42. A hypermarket is a very large store carrying both food and non-food items.

[244] Planet Retail database (accessed April 12, 2011). For all countries, modern grocery distribution is divided by Planet Retail into several categories: "modern retail formats predominantly selling food" (e.g., supermarkets, superstores, and convenience stores); "mixed merchandise retail formats operated by grocery retail groups... predominately selling non-food," such as department and variety stores; "non-food retail banners operated by grocery retail groups;" and "modern wholesale formats," such as warehouse clubs. Because cash-and-carry and delivered wholesale sales are included, these data are not directly comparable to the overall retail sales cited above.

[245] Figuié and Moustier, "Market Appeal in an Emerging Economy," April 2009. The authors surveyed households in a working-class neighborhood of Hanoi and found that less than 3 percent of low-income households shopped regularly at supermarkets. The authors quote a 2006 study which found that 10 percent of the poor in Ho Chi Minh City shopped regularly in supermarkets (Phan Thi, "Poor Consumers' Access," 2006).

[246] World Bank, World Development Indicators database. The quoted figure is in 2005 international purchasing power parity prices (i.e., it is based on how much money is needed to purchase the same goods and services in different countries).

[247] Maruyama and Trung, "Traditional Bazaar or Supermarkets," July 2007, 248. Prices in supermarkets are often higher than in traditional markets in the early stages of supermarket penetration, but as chains expand and achieve economies of scale, those prices fall (Figuié and Moustier, "Market Appeal in an Emerging Economy," 2009, 2). A study published in 2008 suggested that prices for fresh fruits and vegetables generally remained higher in supermarkets than in traditional outlets in the countries of the authors' "third wave of supermarket diffusion," of which Vietnam is a member (Reardon and Gulati, "The Supermarket Revolution," June 2008, 1).

[248] WTO, "Viet Nam," March 19, 2007. Tobacco, print media, video, precious stones, pharmaceuticals, explosives, oil, rice, and sugar were excluded from the commitments.

[249] Vietnam's regulations also require the Ministry of Industry and Trade (MOIT) to approve a foreign retailer's initial outlet, but the regulations do not specify the criteria that MOIT uses for such approvals. This may violate Article VI.5 of the GATS, which requires licenses to be issued based on "objective and transparent criteria."

[250] WTO, "Viet Nam," March 19, 2007.

[251] Circular 09/2007/QD-BTM (Amended by Circular 05/2008/TT-BCT) and Decision 10/2007/QD-BTM. At the time of the writing of this study, Vietnam was drafting a new retail decree to supersede the present ENT regulations. Early drafts that were released publicly in fall 2010 did not resolve the concerns noted above.

[252] Representatives of donor-funded technical assistance programs, interview by USITC staff, Hanoi, Vietnam, December 7, 2010.

[253] According to a media report, the official, Hoang Tho Xuan of the MOIT's Domestic Market Department, said "under current regulations, foreign retail distributors are still required to sell through a single retail outlet, and it isn't easy to set up a second outlet." *VNS*, "Domestic Distributors Need Not Be Afraid," January 3, 2009.

[254] Representatives of donor-funded technical assistance programs, interview by USITC staff, Hanoi, Vietnam, December7, 2010.

[255] A media report about the decision speculated on the reasons for the rejection (such as the presence of other large retail outlets in the proposed shopping center's neighborhood), but gave no indication that a clear explanation accompanied the decision. Hung, "Plan for Second Lotte Mart in City Rejected," May 6, 2009.

[256] Nguyen and Dapice, "Vietnam's Infrastructure Constraints," February 2009, 2.

[257] World Bank, "2010 Logistics Performance Index," 2010.

[258] USAID and VNCI, "Vietnam Provincial Competitiveness Index 2009," 2009, 26.

[259] Planet Retail, "Country Report: Vietnam," April 6, 2011, 21.

[260] The authors heard about this problem from the business community repeatedly during field research in Vietnam for a separate study in March 2010.

[261] Maruyama and Trung, "Modern Retailers in Transition Economies," March 10, 2011, 26.

[262] Vietnam government official, correspondence with USITC staff, September 26, 2011.

[263] Maruyama and Trung, "Modern Retailers in Transition Economies," March 10, 2011, 20, 50–51.

[264] World Bank, Investing Across Borders Database.

[265] Cushman & Wakefield, *Main Streets across the World 2010*, 2010, 8–9.

[266] Ibid., 15.

[267] Cushman & Wakefield, "Hanoi Retail Report," April 12, 2011, 2.

[268] Planet Retail, "New Dawn for Vietnam's Retail Sector," January 9, 2009.

[269] Planet Retail database (accessed April 13, 2011); Metro Cash & Carry Vietnam, "Background and History," n.d. (accessed September 12, 2011).

[270] For example, in 2010, Casino entered the provinces of Nam Dinh, Vinh Phuc, and Nghe An, while Metro entered Binh Dinh, An Giang, and Binh Duong.

[271] *VietNamNet Bridge*, "Retailers Following 'Expansionism' in Vietnam's Market," March 4, 2011.

[272] Ibid.; Planet Retail database (accessed April 13, 2011).

[273] The ownership structure of many Vietnamese companies is opaque. For example, Saigon Co-op's Web site describes the company as "an economic co-operative organization owned by the community." Planet Retail acknowledges the role of cooperatives in its ownership but also characterizes it as "state-owned." It is possible that the Vietnamese state holds significant ownership stakes in other leading domestic retailers, but the extent of its stakes is not clear from publicly available information. Planet Retail database (accessed April 13, 2011); Saigon Co-op Mart, "History" (accessed April 13, 2011).

[274] *VietNamNet Bridge*, "Saigon Co.op Touches on Shopping Mall," March 9, 2010.

[275] The 2009 population was about 86 million; many Vietnamese subscribe to multiple telephone lines, as discussed below.

[276] ITU, World Telecommunication/ICT Indicators 2010 database.

[277] Hot Telecom, *Country Profile*, May 2011, 10.

[278] Government of Vietnam, MIC, *Viet Nam Information and Communication Technology White Book 2010*, 2010, 39.

[279] Paul Budde Communication, *Vietnam*, August 3, 2011, 9.

[280] Ibid., 8.

[281] The creation of the MIC was driven in large part by Vietnam's WTO accession commitments in telecommunication services. In 2002, the Ministry of Posts and Telematics replaced an older regulatory body, the Directorate General of Posts and Telecommunications. Important units within MIC related to telecommunication services include the Department of Telecommunications (DOT); the Radio Frequency Department (RFD); and the Vietnam Internet Network Information Center.

[282] Government of Vietnam, MIC, "Main Functions," n.d. (accessed September 12, 2011). The MIC is also responsible for functions pertaining to press, publishing, postal, and related public services.

[283] Ibid.

[284] From 2002 through 2010, the Vietnamese telecommunication services industry had been governed by P&T Ordinance No. 43/2002/PL-UBTVQH10 of May 2002. LookAtVietnam, "Five Bills Adopted at NA Session," November 24, 2009.

[285] TeleGeography, *Vietnam*, 2011, 5.

[286] Ibid., 6. The VNTA was formed by merging two agencies within the MIC, the Department of Telecommunications and the Authority of Information and Communication Technology Quality Control.

[287] Ibid., 6.

[288] Decree No. 25/2011/ND-CP of April 6, 2011.

[289] Baker & McKenzie, *Client Alert*, April 2011, 1. This restriction applies only to telecommunication services found in a specific list to be issued by the MIC.

[290] Indochine Counsel, *Client Alert*, April–May 2011, 5–7; Baker & McKenzie, *Client Alert*, April 2011, 2–4.

[291] Paul Budde Communication, *Vietnam,* August 3, 2011, 13.

[292] At the time of writing, seven BCC agreements have been signed in Vietnam's telecommunication services sector, three of which have lapsed. TeleGeography, *Vietnam*, 2011, 7.

[293] Paul Budde Communication, *Vietnam,* August 3, 2011, 13.

[294] Ibid., 13–14.

[295] Industry representative, interview with USITC staff, July 12, 2011. Joint venture arrangements are subject to foreign equity caps.

[296] Industry representative, interview with USITC staff, July 12, 2011.

[297] Local, long-distance, and international telephone calls.

[298] For example, facsimile, mobile telephone, and satellite services.

[299] U.S.-Vietnam Bilateral Trade Agreement, *Annex G, Vietnam*, 2001. Examples of value-added services include Internet, e-mail, and voice mail services.

[300] WTO, "Working Party on the Accession of Viet Nam," October 27, 2006.

[301] TeleGeography, *Vietnam*, 2011, 67–68. Fixed-line voice services in Vietnam are delivered over both wire-line networks and wireless in the local loop networks.

[302] Hot Telecom, *Country Profile*, May 2011, 13; Government of Vietnam, MIC, *Viet Nam Information and Communication Technology White Book 2010*, 2010, 29. By contrast, in 2006, fixed-line penetration was approximately 10 percent. Throughout this section, penetration is determined by calculating the number of telephone lines or subscribers per 100 inhabitants.

[303] World Bank, World Development Indicators database. Economies of similar economic development to Vietnam are defined as countries categorized by the World Bank as lower-

middle-income countries, with the average fixed-line penetration rate calculated using 53 (of 56) countries. Countries not included were Vietnam (as the comparison country) as well as Kosovo and Timor-Leste, due to missing data.

[304] EIU, *Vietnam*, June 16, 2011.

[305] Government of Vietnam, MIC, *Viet Nam Information and Communication Technology White Book 2010*, 2010, 39.

[306] Ibid., 29. VNPT was formed in 1995 when it was separated from the Directorate General of Posts and Telecommunications. In 2003, the Ministry of Posts and Telecommunications (MPT), the regulatory predecessor to MIC, restructured VNPT with the aim of privatizing VNPT's various subsidiaries. Using a "parent-subsidiary" model, in 2005 the MPT created the Vietnam Post and Telecommunications Group and spun off three communications subsidiaries: Telecommunications Corporations I, II, and III, to serve the northern, central, and southern parts of Vietnam, respectively. As part of this restructuring, the MPT also created a postal subsidiary, which was divested from VNPT in 2007, forming Vietnam Post. TeleGeography, *Vietnam*, 2010, 6–7.

[307] TeleGeography, *Vietnam*, 2011, 41. EVN Telecom is a wholly owned subsidiary of another government-controlled utility, Electricity of Vietnam.

[308] Government of Vietnam, MIC, *Viet Nam Information and Communications Technology White Book 2010*, 2010, 41. At the end of 2010, several state-owned enterprises, including VNPT, maintained equity stakes in Saigon Post and Telecommunications. TeleGeography, *Vietnam*, 2011, 76.

[309] TeleGeography, *Vietnam*, 2011, 77. The FPT, a private telecommunications and software company, owns 43.1 percent of FPT Telecom. Remaining shares are owned by the government (50.2 percent) and miscellaneous shareholders (6.7 percent).

[310] As of October 2011, only domestically owned companies offered fixed-line services in Vietnam.

[311] TeleGeography, *Vietnam*, 2011, 67.

[312] Ibid., 12–18. Companies allowed to offer VoIP services in Vietnam include VNPT, EVN Telecom, Viettel, SPT, Hanoi Telecom Company, Vietnam Maritime Communications and Electrics Company, and Indochina Telecom Company.

[313] Government of Vietnam, MIC, *Viet Nam Information and Communication Technology White Book 2010*, 2010, 29.

[314] Economies of similar economic development to Vietnam are defined as countries categorized by the World Bank as lower-middle-income countries, with the average fixed-line penetration rate calculated using 52 (of 56) countries. Countries not included were Vietnam (as the comparison country) as well as Guyana, Kosovo, and Timor-Leste, due to missing data.

[315] SIM cards are portable memory chips that authenticate the identity of the mobile phone subscriber and hold data such as contacts and text messages.

[316] TeleGeography, *Vietnam*, 2011, 12–19. Other efforts by the government to reduce the number of SIM cards include requiring customers to register prepaid SIM cards and restricting marketing and promotional campaigns.

[317] TeleGeography, *Vietnam*, 2011, 39–40. S-Telecom was formed in 2001 when government-owned Saigon Postal and two Korean companies, SK Telecom (SKT) and LG Electronics, received approval to form a 15-year BCC. In December 2009, SKT stopped investing in S-Telecom due to low profits and subscriptions. In 2010, the government of Vietnam approved the transformation of S-Telecom from a BCC to a joint venture, with Saigon Postal and SKT taking stakes of 80 percent and 20 percent, respectively. Saigon Postal

subsequently announced plans to purchase SKT's stake and then sell 20–30 percent of the company to new partners.

[318] Ibid., 37–38. Hanoi Telecom operates in Vietnam under the brand name Vietnamobile. In 2005, Hanoi Telecom received government approval for a 15-year business BCC with Hong Kong-based Hutchinson Telecommunications International Limited (Hutchinson). As of May 2001, Hutchinson had invested more than one billion dollars in Vietnamobile.

[319] Ibid., 43. Vimplecom, a mobile services company based in Russia, owns 49 percent of GTel, giving it management control of the company. Remaining shares are owned by the government-owned Global Telecommunications Corporation. Vimplecom has initiated a two-year financing plan which is scheduled to increase its ownership share to 65 percent by the end of 2013.

[320] Government of Vietnam, MIC, *Viet Nam Information and Communication Technology White Book 2010*, 2010, 39–41. An eighth company, Cityphone, operated exclusively in Hanoi and Ho Chi Minh City. By August 2010, Cityphone had attracted only 30,000 customers, largely due to geographic restrictions and reliance on outdated technology (iPAS). In 2010, parent company VNPT ceased operations in Ho Chi Minh City and announced plans to end the service in Hanoi. TeleGeography, *Vietnam*, 2011, 43–44.

[321] Mobile virtual network operators offer mobile telecommunication services by purchasing wholesale voice minutes and/or leasing network capacity from mobile service providers that own and operate physical network infrastructure.

[322] Government of Vietnam, MIC, *Viet Nam Information and Communication Technology White Book 2010*, 2010, 39, 41; TeleGeography, *Vietnam*, 2011, 21.

[323] TeleGeography, *Vietnam*, 2011, 9–10.

[324] Ibid., 21. As of August 2011, Viettel, Vinaphone, and MobiFone had not requested permission from MIC to reduce prices.

[325] Ibid., 11. GTel and S-Fone are permitted to offer 3G services over the networks of the four license winners.

[326] Government of Vietnam, MIC, *Viet Nam Information and Communication Technology White Book 2010*, 2010, 29.

[327] Although concessions were awarded on a technology-neutral basis, Long Term Evolution is expected to be the 4G technology of choice.

[328] TeleGeography, *Vietnam*, 2011, 11.

[329] ITU, World Telecommunication/ICT Indicators 2010 database.

[330] Government of Vietnam, MIC, *Viet Nam Information and Communications Technology White Book 2010,* 2010, 31; Hot Telecom, *Country Profile*, May 2011, 10. According to MIC, there were approximately 4.8 million computers in Vietnam at the end of 2009, representing a penetration rate of approximately 5 percent.

[331] Government of Vietnam, MIC, *Viet Nam Information and Communications Technology White Book 2010*, 2010, 31.

[332] TeleGeography, *Vietnam*, 2011, 14–15. In 2010, MIC revoked seven ISP licenses, largely because Internet services had not been initiated in the two years after the licenses were issued.

[333] Government of Vietnam, MIC, *Viet Nam Information and Communications Technology White Book 2010*, 2010, 41.

[334] TeleGeography, *Vietnam*, 2011, 15.

[335] Intellectual property refers to creations of the mind and is broadly categorized into two types: industrial property, such as inventions, trademarks, and industrial designs, and artistic products, such as novels, films, and music. WIPO, "What Is Intellectual Property?" n.d.

(accessed September 12, 2011). Both IPR and IP (intellectual property) are discussed in this analysis. IP refers to the property itself and IPR to the rights associated with the property. USITC, *China*, 2010, 1-2.

[336] All WTO members are signatories to the TRIPS agreement. For additional information on the TRIPS agreement within the WTO Framework, see Hunter Rodwell Consulting, "Intellectual Property Rights Primer for Vietnam," June 2008, 13.

[337] Government of Vietnam, Inspectorate of Science and Technology, "Introduction to the IP Administration System of Vietnam," March 25, 2008, 3.

[338] For example, criminal penalties were established for "commercial scale" infringements. USDOC, *Doing Business in Vietnam,* 2011; EIU, *Country Commerce*, 2010, 90. However, as of the time of writing the implementing decrees and regulations have not yet been enacted. U.S. government official, telephone interview by USITC staff, July 27, 2010.

[339] The WIPO is an agency of the United Nations that "is dedicated to developing a balanced and accessible international intellectual property system." WIPO Web site. http://www.wipo.int//about-wipo/en/what_is_wipo.html (accessed September 12, 2011).

[340] Ibid.

[341] International Convention for the Protection of New Varieties of Plants, "Members of the International Union for the Protection of New Varieties of Plants," http://www.upov.int/export/sites/upov/members/en/pdf/pub423.pdf (accessed August 13, 2012).

[342] For a summary of obligations under the BTA, see U.S.-Vietnam Trade Council, "Summary of the Agreement between the U.S. and Vietnam on Trade Relations," May 10, 2004. According to the International Intellectual Property Alliance, Vietnam was not in full compliance with its BTA commitments as of 2011. IIPA, written submission, February 15, 2011, 141.

[343] Government of Vietnam, Inspectorate of Science and Technology, "Introduction to the IP Administration System of Vietnam," March 25, 2008.

[344] For example, the Copyright Office of Vietnam was established in 2003. Government of Vietnam, COV website.

[345] U.S. government official, telephone interview by USITC staff, July 27, 2011.

[346] Vietnam ranks 51st out of 123 countries for an aggregate measure of innovation, and ranks 85th in terms of human capital and research. INSEAD. "The Global Innovation Index 2011," 2011.

[347] Government of Vietnam, Inspectorate of Science and Technology, "Introduction to the IP Administration System of Vietnam," March 25, 2008, 3. The data on domestic trademark filers do not specify the origin of the trademark. Government of Vietnam, NOIP, "Intellectual Property Activities," April 2011.

[348] Examples of counterfeiting affecting Vietnamese trademark owners were noted in taxi services as well as the dairy and coffee sectors. U.S. government official, telephone interview by USITC staff, August 2, 2011.

[349] IACC, written submission to USTR, February 15, 2011, 66; USDOC, U.S. Commercial Service, *Doing Business in Vietnam*, 2011.

[350] USTR, "Vietnam," 2011, 380.

[351] Online piracy is partly driven by improvements in Internet connectivity and capacity. USTR, *Special 301 Report*, 2011, 41.

[352] USDOC, U.S. Commercial Service, "Vietnam: How to Market Products and Services" (accessed June 13, 2011).

[353] IIPA, written submission to USTR, February 15, 2011, 140; IACC, written submission to USTR, February 15, 2011, 66.

[354] EIU, *Country Commerce*, 2011, 94. According to the Motion Picture Association of America (MPAA), the majority of pirated CDs in Vietnam are imported from China. MPAA, "Trade Barriers to Exports of U.S. Filmed Entertainment," November 2009.

[355] Hunter Rodwell Consulting, "Intellectual Property Rights Primer for Vietnam," June 2008, 13.

[356] IIPA, written submission to USTR, February 15, 2011, 137–38.

[357] USTR, *Special 301 Report*, 2011, 41–42; USDOC, U.S. Commercial Service, *Doing Business in Vietnam,* 2011. Several Vietnamese government ministries and sub-agencies have enforcement responsibilities, including the Inspectorate Offices of the Ministry of Science and Technology, the Ministry of Culture and Information, the Ministry of Trade Market Management Bureau, the Ministry of Public Security Economic Police, the Ministry of Finance Customs Office, and the People's Court (Civil Court).

[358] U.S. government official, telephone interview by USITC staff, July 27, 2011. Large-scale IPR infringements with a health or safety component are handled by the Economic Police; copyright infringement is generally handled by the Inspectorate of Culture and Information; and Customs monitors borders for infringing products. Hunter Rodwell Consulting, "Intellectual Property Rights Primer for Vietnam," June 2008, 19.

[359] Government of Vietnam, Inspectorate of Science and Technology, "Introduction to the IP Administration System of Vietnam," March 25, 2008, 3; Hunter Rodwell Consulting, "Intellectual Property Rights Primer for Vietnam," June 2008, 13. U.S. government official, telephone interview by USITC staff, August 2, 2011.

[360] IACC, written submission to USTR, February 15, 2011, 68.

[361] U.S. government official, telephone interview by USITC staff, July 27, 2011.

[362] Hunter Rodwell Consulting, "Intellectual Property Rights Primer for Vietnam," June 2008.

[363] Ibid, 20.

[364] IIPA, written submission to USTR, February 15, 2011, 137; U.S. government official, telephone interview by USITC staff, July 27, 2011.

[365] Commission on Intellectual Property Rights, "Integrating Intellectual Property Rights and Development Policy," November 2002, 158.

[366] Maskus, *International Property Rights in the Global Economy*, 2000, 129.

[367] Strong IP rights raise the cost of IP-protected goods and decrease access to innovation. Branstetter, Foley, and Saggi, "Has the Shift to Intellectual Property Rights Promoted Technology Transfer?" 2010; Maskus, *Intellectual Property Rights in the Global Economy*, 2000, 129.

[368] Cepeda, Lippoldt, and Senft, "Policy Complements to the Strengthening of IPRs," September 14, 2010.

[369] In 2009, during the global recession, trade in services and goods declined for most countries. Government of Vietnam, General Statistics Office, "Exports and Imports of Services," and "Export and Imports of Goods" (accessed June 1, 2011).

[370] In 2010, Vietnam ranked fifth among ASEAN countries in terms of FDI stocks, behind Singapore, Thailand, Indonesia, and Malaysia. UN, UNCTAD STAT (accessed September 12, 2011).

[371] Financial Times, FDI Markets database (accessed September 12, 2011).

[372] Nystedt, "Intel Opens $1 Billion Chip Factory in Vietnam," October 29, 2010.

[373] Park and Lippoldt, "Technology Transfer," January 25, 2008.

[374] Many multinational firms employ a "China plus one" investment strategy, diversifying their supply chains while maintaining China as a manufacturing hub. U.S. government official, telephone interview by USITC staff, August 2, 2011.

[375] Commission on Intellectual Property Rights, "Integrating Intellectual Property Rights and Development Policy," November 2002, 4.

[376] Cepeda, Lippoldt, and Senft, "Policy Complements to the Strengthening of IPRs," September 14, 2010.

[377] Commission on Intellectual Property Rights, "Integrating Intellectual Property Rights and Development Policy," November 2002; SRRC, *Media Piracy in Emerging Economies*, 2011, 16–17. Business software piracy rates in Vietnam are among the highest in the world at 83 percent. GSA, *Eighth Annual BSA Global Software Piracy Report*, May 2011, 3. There are reports that pirated business software is used in government offices. U.S. government official, interview by USITC staff, July 27, 2011.

[378] For example, in China, producing and marketing counterfeit goods is an integral part of many local economies. USITC, hearing transcript, June 15, 2010 (testimony of Daniel Chow, Drake University).

[379] U.S. government official, telephone interview by USITC staff, July 27, 2011.

[380] U.S. government official, telephone interview by USITC staff, August 2, 2011.

[381] A number of artistic groups such as musicians and writers in Vietnam are organized as Artistic Collective Management Organizations, which seek protection of their artistic works. U.S. government official, telephone interview by USITC staff, August 2, 2011. The Vietnam Center for Protection of Music Copyright (VCPMC) is a nonprofit affiliate of the Vietnamese Musicians Association. Its mission includes protecting copyrights of Vietnamese and international musicians by negotiating contracts, collecting fees, and carrying out other related services. VCPMC Web site [in Vietnamese] (accessed September 12, 2011).

In: Vietnam: Service Sector Growth
Editor: Rhett R. Murphy
ISBN: 978-1-62417-549-7

Chapter 2

VIETNAM: COUNTRY PROFILE*

U.S. Department of State

Official Name: Socialist Republic of Vietnam.

* This is an edited, reformatted and augmented version The United States Department of State publication, http://www.state.gov/ r/pa/ei/bgn/4130.htm, dated January 2012.

PROFILE

Geography

Area: 331,114 sq. km. (127,243 sq. mi.); equivalent in size to Ohio, Kentucky, and Tennessee combined. Cities (2009): *Capital*--Hanoi (pop. 6.472 million). *Other cities*--Ho Chi Minh City (formerly Saigon; pop. 7.163 million), Haiphong (pop. 1.841 million), Danang (pop. 890,500), Can Tho (pop. 1.189 million). Terrain: Varies from mountainous to coastal delta. Climate: Tropical monsoon.

People

Nationality: *Noun and adjective*--Vietnamese (sing. and pl.). Population (2011): 90 million. Annual population growth rate (2011): 1.077%. Ethnic groups (2009): 54 groups including Vietnamese (Kinh) (73.594 million, or 85.7% of the population), Tay (1.89%), Thai (1.8%), Muong (1.47%), Khmer (1.46%), Chinese (0.95%), Nung (1.12%), Hmong (1.24%).

Religions (2008): Buddhism (approx. 50%), Catholicism (8%-10%), Cao Dai (1.5%-3%), Protestantism (0.5%-2%), Hoa Hao (1.5%-4%), Islam (0.1%), and other animist religions.

Languages: Vietnamese (official), English (increasingly favored as a second language), some French, Chinese, and other ethnic minority languages.

Education (2009): *Literacy*--94%. Health (2011): *Birth rate*--17.07 births/1,000 population. *Infant mortality rate*--20.9 deaths/1,000 live births. *Life expectancy*--73 yrs. *Death rate*--5.96/1,000 population.

Government

Type: Single-party constitutional republic (Communist Party). Independence: September 2, 1945. Constitution: April 15, 1992. Branches: *Executive*--president (head of state and chair of National Defense and Security Council) and prime minister (heads cabinet of ministries and commissions). *Legislative*--National Assembly. *Judicial*--Supreme People's Court; Prosecutorial Supreme People's Procuracy. Administrative subdivisions: 58 provinces, 5 municipalities (Can Tho, Haiphong, Danang, Hanoi, Ho Chi Minh City).

Political party: Communist Party of Vietnam (CPV) with over 3 million members, formerly (1951-76) Vietnam Worker's Party, itself the successor of the Indochinese Communist Party founded in 1930. Suffrage: Universal over 18.

Economy

GDP: (2010) $102 billion; (2011, first 9 months) $81 billion. Real GDP growth rate: (2010) 6.8%; (2011, first 9 months) 5.76%. Per capita income (2010): US $1,168. Inflation rate: 9.2% (average monthly Consumer Price Index of 2010, year-on-year); 18.16% (average monthly Consumer Price Index of first 9 months of 2011, year-on-year).External debt (2010): 42.2% of GDP, $32.50 billion.

Natural resources: Coal, crude oil, zinc, copper, silver, gold, manganese, iron.

Agriculture, forestry, and fisheries (20.58% of GDP, 2010): *Principal products*--rice, coffee, cashews, maize, pepper (spice), sweet potato, pork, peanuts, plus extensive aquaculture of both fish and shellfish species. *Cultivated land*--12.2 million hectares. *Land use*--21% arable; 28% forest and woodland; 51% other.

Industry and construction (41.09% of GDP, 2010): *Principal types*--mining and quarrying, manufacturing, electricity, gas, crude oil, water supply, cement, coal, and steel.

Services (38.33% of GDP, 2010): *Principal types*--tourism, wholesale and retail, repair of vehicles and personal goods, hotel and restaurant, transport storage, telecommunications.

Trade: *Exports*--(2010) $71.6 billion; (2011, first 9 months) $70 billion. *Principal exports*--crude oil, garments/textiles, footwear, fishery and seafood products, rice (world's second-largest exporter), pepper (spice; world's largest exporter), wood products, coffee, rubber, cashews, jewelry, and footwear. *Major export partners*--US, EU, ASEAN, Japan, China, and South Korea. *Imports*--(2010) $84 billion; (2011, first 9 months) $76.87 billion. *Principal imports*--machinery, oil and gas, iron and steel, garment materials, plastics, and electronics. *Major import partners*--China, ASEAN, Japan, Taiwan, South Korea, and EU. *Exports to US*--(2010) $14.3 billion; (2011, first 9 months) $10.9 billion. *Imports from US*--(2010) 3.7 billion; (2011, first 9 months) $2.8 billion.

People

Originating in what is now southern China and northern Vietnam, the Vietnamese people pushed southward over 2 millennia to occupy the entire eastern seacoast of the Indochinese Peninsula. Vietnam has 54 ethnic groups; ethnic Vietnamese or Kinh constitute approximately 85% of Vietnam's population. The next largest groups are ethnic Tay and Thai, which account for 1.89% and 1.8% of Vietnam's population and are concentrated in the country's northern highlands.

With a population of more than 900,000, Vietnam's Chinese community has historically played an important role in the Vietnamese economy. Restrictions on economic activity following reunification of the north and south in 1975 and a general deterioration in Vietnamese-Chinese relations caused increasing anxiety within the Chinese-Vietnamese community. As tensions between Vietnam and China reached their peak in 1978-79, culminating in a brief but bloody war in February-March 1979, some 450,000 ethnic Chinese left Vietnam by boat as refugees (many officially encouraged and assisted) or were expelled across the land border with China.

Other significant ethnic minority groups include central highland peoples (formerly collectively termed Montagnards) such as the Gia Rai, Bana, Ede, Xo Dang, Gie Trieng, and the Khmer Krom (Cambodians), who are concentrated near the Cambodian border and at the mouth of the Mekong River. Taken collectively, these groups made up a majority of the population in much of Vietnam's central highlands until the 1960s and 1970s. They now compose a significant minority of 25% to 35% of the provinces in that region.

Vietnamese is the official language of the country. It is a tonal language with influences from Thai, Khmer, and Chinese. Since the early 20th century, the Vietnamese have used a Romanized script introduced by the French. Previously, Chinese characters and an indigenous phonetic script were both used.

History

Vietnam's identity has been shaped by long-running conflicts, both internally and with foreign forces. In 111 BC, China's Han dynasty conquered northern Vietnam's Red River Delta and the ancestors of today's Vietnamese. Chinese dynasties ruled Vietnam for the next 1,000 years, inculcating it with Confucian ideas and political culture, but also leaving a tradition of resistance to foreign occupation. In 939 AD, Vietnam achieved independence under a native dynasty. After 1471, when Vietnam conquered the Champa Kingdom in what is now central Vietnam, the Vietnamese moved gradually southward, finally reaching the agriculturally rich Mekong Delta, where they encountered previously settled communities of Cham and Cambodians. As Vietnam's Le dynasty declined, powerful northern and southern families, the Trinh and Nguyen, fought civil wars in the 17th and 18th centuries. A peasant revolt originating in the Tay Son region of central Vietnam defeated both the Nguyen and the Trinh and unified the country at the end of the 18th century, but was itself defeated by a surviving member of the Nguyen family, who founded the Nguyen dynasty as Emperor Gia Long in 1802.

French Rule and the Anti-Colonial Struggle

In 1858, the French began their conquest of Vietnam starting in the south. They annexed all of Vietnam in 1885, governing the territories of Annan, Tonkin, and Cochin China, together with Cambodia and Laos, as French Indochina. The French ruled Cochin China directly as a French colony; Annan and Tonkin were established as French "protectorates." Vietnam's emperors remained in place in Hue, but their authority was strictly limited as French officials assumed nearly all government functions. In the early 20th century, Vietnamese intellectuals, many of them French educated, organized nationalist and communist-nationalist anti-colonial movements.

Japan's military occupation of Vietnam during World War II further stirred nationalist sentiment, as well as antipathy toward the French Vichy colonial regime, which took its direction from the Japanese until the Japanese took direct control in March 1945. Vietnamese communists under Ho Chi Minh organized a coalition of anti-colonial groups, the Viet Minh, though many anti-communists refused to join. The Viet Minh took advantage of political uncertainty in the weeks following Japan's surrender to take control of Hanoi and much of northern Vietnam. Ho Chi Minh announced the independence of the Democratic Republic of Vietnam on September 2, 1945.

North and South Partition

France's determination to reassert colonial authority in Vietnam led to failed talks and, after armed hostilities broke out in Haiphong at the end of 1946, an 8-year guerrilla war between the communist-led Viet Minh on one side and the French and their anti-communist nationalist allies on the other. Following the French defeat at Dien Bien Phu in May 1954, France and other parties, including Britain, China, the Soviet Union, the United States, and representatives of the Viet Minh and Bao Dai governments convened in Geneva, Switzerland for peace talks. On July 29, 1954, an Agreement on the Cessation of Hostilities in Vietnam was signed between France and the Democratic Republic of Vietnam. The United States observed, but did not sign, the agreement. French colonial rule in Vietnam ended.

The 1954 Geneva agreement provided for a cease-fire between communist and anti-communist nationalist forces, the temporary division of Vietnam at approximately the 17th parallel, provisional northern (communist) and southern (noncommunist) zone governments, and the evacuation of anti-communist Vietnamese from northern to southern Vietnam, as well as the movement of a smaller number of former communist-led Viet Minh anti-colonial fighters to the north. The agreement also called for an election to be held by July 1956 to bring the two provisional zones under a unified government, a provision that the South Vietnamese Government refused to accept, arguing that conditions for free elections throughout Vietnam were not present. On October 26, 1955, South Vietnam declared itself the Republic of Vietnam.

After 1954, North Vietnamese communist leaders consolidated their power and instituted a harsh agrarian reform and socialization program. During this period, some 450,000 Vietnamese, including a large number of Vietnamese Catholics, fled from the north to the south, while a much smaller number, mostly consisting of former Viet Minh fighters, relocated north. In the late 1950s, North Vietnamese leaders reactivated the network of communist guerrillas that had remained behind in the south. These forces--commonly known as the Viet Cong--aided covertly by the north, started an armed campaign against officials and villagers who refused to support the communist reunification cause.

American Assistance to the South

In December 1961, at the request of South Vietnamese President Ngo Dinh Diem, President Kennedy sent US military advisers to South Vietnam to help the government there deal with the Viet Cong campaign. In the wake of escalating political turmoil in the south after a November 1963 generals' coup against President Diem, which resulted in his death, the United States increased its military support for South Vietnam. In March 1965, President Johnson sent the first US combat forces to Vietnam. The American military role peaked in 1969 with an in-country force of 534,000. Although the Viet Cong's surprise Tet Offensive in January 1968 failed militarily, it damaged American and South Vietnamese morale and brought into question--

domestically--US reports of successes prior to the offensive. In January 1969, the United States, governments of South and North Vietnam, and the Viet Cong met for the first plenary session of peace talks in Paris, France. These talks, which began with much hope, moved slowly. They finally concluded with the signing of a peace agreement, the Paris Accords, on January 27, 1973. The Accords called for a ceasefire in place in which North Vietnamese forces were permitted to remain in areas they controlled. Following the Accords, the South Vietnamese Government and the political representatives of the communist forces in the South, the Provisional Revolutionary Government, vied for control over portions of South Vietnam. The United States withdrew its forces, although reduced levels of US military assistance continued, administered by the Defense Attaché Office.

Reunification

In early 1975, North Vietnamese regular military forces began a major offensive in the south, inflicting great damage to the south's forces. The communists took Saigon on April 30, 1975, and announced their intention to reunify the country. The Democratic Republic of Vietnam (north) absorbed the former Republic of Vietnam (south) to form the Socialist Republic of Vietnam on July 2, 1976.

After reunification, the government confiscated privately owned land and forced citizens to adopt collectivized agricultural practices. Hundreds of thousands of former South Vietnamese government and military officials, as well as intellectuals previously opposed to the communist cause, were sent to study socialist doctrine in re-education camps, where they remained for periods ranging from months to over 10 years.

Expectations that reunification of the country and its socialist transformation would be condoned by the international community were quickly dashed as many countries expressed concern over Vietnam's internal practices and foreign policy. Vietnam's 1978 invasion of Cambodia in particular, together with its increasingly tight alliance with the Soviet Union, appeared to confirm suspicions that Vietnam wanted to establish a Soviet-backed hegemony in Indochina.

Vietnam's invasion of Cambodia also heightened tensions that had been building between Vietnam and China. Beijing, which backed the Khmer Rouge regime in Cambodia, retaliated in early 1979 by initiating a brief, but bloody border war with Vietnam.

Vietnam's tensions with its neighbors, internal repression, and a stagnant economy contributed to a massive exodus from Vietnam. Fearing persecution, many ethnic Chinese in particular fled Vietnam by boat to nearby countries. Later, hundreds of thousands of other Vietnamese nationals fled as well, seeking temporary refuge in camps throughout Southeast Asia.

The continuing grave condition of the economy and the alienation from the international community became focal points of party debate. In 1986, at the Sixth Party Congress, there was an important easing of communist agrarian and commercial policies.

Government and Political Conditions

A new state constitution was approved in April 1992, reaffirming the central role of the Communist Party of Vietnam (CPV) in politics and society, and outlining government reorganization and increased economic freedom. Though Vietnam remains a one-party state, adherence to ideological orthodoxy has become less important than economic development as a national priority.

The most important powers within the Vietnamese Government--in addition to the Communist Party--are the executive agencies created by the 1992 constitution: the offices of the president and the prime minister. The Vietnamese President functions as head of state but also serves as the nominal commander of the armed forces and chairman of the Council on National Defense and Security. The Prime Minister of Vietnam heads a cabinet composed of deputy prime ministers and the heads of ministries and agencies, all confirmed by the National Assembly.

Notwithstanding the 1992 constitution's reaffirmation of the central role of the Communist Party, the National Assembly, according to the constitution, is the highest representative body of the people and the only organization with legislative powers. It has a broad mandate to oversee all government functions. Once seen as little more than a rubber stamp, the National Assembly has become more vocal and assertive in exercising its authority over lawmaking, particularly in recent years. However, the National Assembly is still subject to Communist Party direction. More than 90% of the deputies in the National Assembly are Communist Party members. The National Assembly meets twice yearly for 7-10 weeks each time; elections for members are held every 5 years, although its Standing Committee meets monthly and there are now over 140 "full-time" deputies who function on various committees. In 2007, the National Assembly introduced parliamentary "question time," in which cabinet ministers must answer often-pointed questions from National Assembly members. There is a separate judicial branch, but it is still relatively weak. There are few lawyers and trial procedures are rudimentary.

The Politburo, selected during the Party Congress of the Communist Party of Vietnam and headed by the Communist Party General Secretary, determines government policy; its Secretariat oversees day-to-day policy implementation. In addition, the Communist Party's Central Military Commission, which is composed of select Politburo members and additional military leaders, determines military policy.

A Party Congress meets every 5 years to set the direction of the party and the government. The most recent Party Congress, the Eleventh, met in January 2011. The Central Committee is elected by the Party Congress and usually meets at least twice a year.

Principal Government Officials

President-- Truong Tan Sang
Prime Minister--Nguyen Tan Dung
National Assembly Chairman--Nguyen Sinh Hung
Minister of Foreign Affairs--Pham Binh Minh
Ambassador to the United States--Nguyen Quoc Cuong
Ambassador to the United Nations--Le Hoai Trung

Vietnam maintains an embassy in the US at 1233 20th Street, NW, #400, Washington DC 20036 (tel. 202-861-0737; fax 202-861-0917); Internet home page: www.vietnamembassy-usa.org. There is a consulate general in San Francisco, located at 1700 California Street, Suite 430, San Francisco, CA 94109 (tel. 415-922-1707; fax 415-922-1848); Internet homepage: http://www.vietnamconsulate-sf.org. There also is a consulate general in Houston, located at 5251 Westheimer Rd, Suite 1100, Houston, Texas 77056 (tel. 713-850-1233; fax 713-810-0159); Internet homepage: http://vietnamconsulatein houston.org.

Economy

Following economic stagnation after reunification from 1975 to 1985, the 1986 Sixth Party Congress approved broad economic reforms (known as "Doi Moi," or "renovation") that introduced market reforms, opened up the country for foreign investment, and dramatically improved Vietnam's business climate. Vietnam became one of the fastest-growing economies in the world, averaging around 8% annual gross domestic product (GDP) growth from 1990 to 1997 and 6.5% from 1998-2003. GDP grew more than 8% annually from 2004 to 2007, slowed to 5.3% growth in 2009, recovered to 6.8% in 2010, and reached 5.8% over the first 9 months of 2011. Viewed over time, foreign trade and foreign direct investment (FDI) have improved significantly, although new registered FDI has started to trend downward. The average annual foreign investment commitment rose sharply after foreign investment was authorized in 1988, although the global economic crisis affected FDI in 2009. In the first 9 months of 2011, disbursed FDI capital totaled $9.1 billion, up 1% compared to the same period in 2010. Registered FDI (including new and additional capital) was $8.88 billion in the first 9 months of 2011, a fall of about 30% compared to the same period of 2010. From 1990 to 2011, agricultural production nearly doubled, transforming Vietnam from a net food importer to the world's second-largest exporter of rice. In the first 9 months of 2011, Vietnam's exports ($70 billion) were up by 23% compared to the same period in 2010. Vietnam's imports ($76.87 billion) were up by 27% from the same period in 2010, and the country was still running a structural trade deficit, reaching $6.87 billion in the first 9 months of 2011.

The shift away from a centrally planned economy to a more market-oriented economic model has improved the quality of life for many Vietnamese. Per capita income rose from $220 in 1994 to $1,168 in 2010. Year-on-year inflation, however, increased to 18.2% in the first 9 months of 2011, up from 8.6% in the same period of 2010. The Vietnamese Government was unable to reach its 2011 Consumer Price Index (CPI) target of 7%. The Vietnamese savings rate is about 25% of GDP. Official unemployment remains low, but does not reflect employment trends in the unofficial economy, which comprises over 70% of the total workforce. Unemployment was 2.2% in the first 9 months of 2011--a slight decline from 2.8% in 2010--with urban unemployment being higher (3.5% in the first 9 months of 2011, 4.4% in 2010) than rural (1.2% the first 9 months of 2011, 2.3% in 2010).

The Vietnamese Government still holds a tight rein over major sectors of the economy through large state-owned economic groups and enterprises. The government has plans to reform key sectors and partially privatize state-owned enterprises, but implementation has been gradual and the state sector still accounts for approximately 40% of GDP. Greater emphasis on private sector development is critical for job creation. In 2011, the Vietnamese Government proposed a strategy for restructuring the economy by 2015. The three pillars of the proposed strategy are improving public investment; reforming state-owned enterprises; and restructuring finance markets, focusing on the banking system.

The 2001 entry-into-force of the Bilateral Trade Agreement (BTA) between the US and Vietnam was a significant milestone for Vietnam's economy and for normalization of US-Vietnam relations. Bilateral trade between the United States and Vietnam has expanded dramatically, rising from $2.97 billion in 2002 to $18.6 billion in 2010. The US is Vietnam's second-largest trade partner overall (after China).

Implementation of the BTA, which includes provisions on trade in goods and services, enforcement of intellectual property rights, protection for investments, and transparency, fundamentally changed Vietnam's trade regime and helped it accede to the World Trade Organization (WTO) in 2007.

Vietnam was granted permanent normal trade relations (PNTR) status by the United States in December 2006. To meet the obligations of WTO membership, Vietnam revised nearly all of its trade and investment laws and guiding regulations and opened up large sectors of its economy to foreign investors and exporters.

A US-Vietnam Trade and Investment Framework Agreement (TIFA), a bridge to future economic cooperation, was signed in 2007 during President Nguyen Minh Triet's visit to the United States. The first TIFA Council occurred in December 2007 in Washington, and there have been frequent TIFA meetings and dialogues since then. During Prime Minister Nguyen Tan Dung's June 2008 visit, the United States and Vietnam committed to undertake Bilateral Investment Treaty (BIT) negotiations. Three rounds of talks were completed, but BIT talks have not resumed since Vietnam and the United States began negotiations on free trade in 2010.

Agriculture and Industry

As in the rest of Asia, farms in Vietnam tend to be very small, and are usually less than one hectare (2.5 acres) each. Rice and other farm outputs are quite profitable, on a per-kilogram basis, but the total income from these small operations is increasingly insufficient to cover daily household needs. Off-farm income is necessary, and growing in importance. Due to its high productivity, Vietnam is currently a net exporter of agricultural products. Besides rice, key exports are coffee (robusta), pepper (spice), cashews, tea, rubber, wood products, and fisheries products. In 2010, Vietnam was ranked

17 among all suppliers of food and agricultural products to the United States, a strong indicator of Vietnam's growing importance as a global supplier of key agricultural commodities. Agriculture's share of economic output has declined, falling as a share of GDP from 42% in 1989 to 21% in 2010, as production in other sectors of the economy has risen.

Vietnam's industrial production has also grown. Industry and construction contributed 41% of GDP in 2010, up from 27.3% in 1985. Subsidies have been cut, though state enterprises still receive priority access to resources, including land and capital. The government is also continuing the slow process of "equitizing" a significant number of smaller state enterprises--transforming state enterprises into shareholding companies and distributing a portion of the shares to management, workers, and private foreign and domestic investors. However, to date the government continues to maintain control of the largest and most important companies.

Trade and Balance of Payments

To compensate for drastic cuts in Soviet-bloc support after 1989, Vietnam liberalized trade, devalued its currency to increase exports, and embarked on a policy of regional and international economic re-integration. Vietnam has demonstrated its commitment to trade liberalization in recent years, and integration with the world economy has become one of the cornerstones of its reform program.

Vietnam has locked in its intention to create a more competitive and open economy by committing to several comprehensive international trade agreements, including the Association of Southeast Asian Nations (ASEAN) Free Trade Area (AFTA) and the US-Vietnam Bilateral Trade Agreement (BTA).

Vietnam's accession to the World Trade Organization further integrated Vietnam into the global economy. In November 2010, Vietnam officially joined negotiations for the Trans-Pacific Partnership (TPP) free trade agreement. As a result of these reforms, exports expanded significantly, growing by as much as 20%-30% in some years. Exports accounted for about 70% of GDP in 2010.

Imports have also grown rapidly, and Vietnam has maintained a structural trade deficit, reaching $12.4 billion in 2010. Vietnam's total external debt, amounting to 42.2% of GDP in 2010, was estimated at around $32.5 billion.

Foreign Relations

During the second Indochina war (1954-75), North Vietnam sought to balance relations with its two major allies, the Soviet Union and China. Tensions with China began to grow during the Chinese Cultural Revolution, and by 1975, Beijing had become increasingly critical of Hanoi's growing ties with Moscow. Over the next 4 years, Beijing's growing support for Cambodia's Khmer Rouge, which in 1978 initiated bloody attacks across its border with Vietnam, reinforced Vietnamese suspicions of China's motives.

Vietnam-China relations deteriorated significantly after Hanoi instituted a ban in March 1978 on private trade, which had a particularly large impact on southern Vietnam's ethnic Chinese community. Following Vietnam's December 1978 invasion of Cambodia and the expulsion of a significant number of Hoa (ethnic Chinese) from Vietnam, China in February 1979 launched a 3-week incursion over Vietnam's northern border. Faced with severance of Chinese aid and strained international relations, Vietnam established even closer ties with the Soviet Union and its allies in the Council for Mutual Economic Assistance (Comecon). Through the 1980s, Vietnam received nearly $3 billion a year in economic and military aid from the Soviet Union and conducted most of its trade with that country and with other Comecon countries. However, Soviet and East bloc economic aid declined during the perestroika era and ceased completely after the breakup of the Soviet Union.

Vietnam did not begin to emerge from international isolation until it withdrew its troops from Cambodia in 1989. Within months of the 1991 Paris Agreements, Vietnam established diplomatic and economic relations with ASEAN, as well as with most of the countries of Western Europe and Northeast Asia. China reestablished full diplomatic ties with Vietnam in 1991, and the two countries began joint efforts to demarcate their land and sea borders, expand trade and investment ties, and build political relations.

Over the past decades, Vietnam has recognized the increasing importance of growing global economic interdependence and has made concerted efforts to adjust its foreign relations to reflect the evolving international economic and political situation in Southeast Asia. The country has begun to integrate itself into the regional and global economy by joining international organizations. Vietnam has stepped up its efforts to attract foreign capital from the West and regularize relations with the world financial system. In the 1990s, following the lifting of the American veto on multilateral loans to the country, Vietnam became a member of the World Bank, the International Monetary Fund, and the Asian Development Bank. The country has expanded trade with its East Asian neighbors as well as with countries in Western Europe and North America. Of particular significance was Vietnam's acceptance into the Association of Southeast Asian Nations (ASEAN) in July 1995. Vietnam's influence in ASEAN has expanded significantly; the country served as Chairman in 2010. Vietnam joined the Asia-Pacific Economic Cooperation forum (APEC) in November 1998 and hosted summits for APEC in 2006 and ASEAN in 2010. In December 2009, Vietnam completed a 2-year term as a non-permanent member of the United Nations Security Council. At the Eleventh Party Congress in 2011, Communist Party leaders adopted a more internationally engaged foreign policy platform, which also called for a more government-wide approach to foreign policy, increasingly involving the Ministry of National Defense and Ministry of Public Security in the policy-making process. While Vietnam has not experienced war since its withdrawal from Cambodia, tensions have periodically flared between Vietnam and China, primarily over boundary issues. While Vietnam and China were able to agree to land borders in 1999, overlapping maritime claims in the South China Sea continue to increase bilateral tensions. Vietnam and China each assert claims to the Spratly and Paracel Islands, archipelagos in the potentially oil-rich area of the South China Sea. Malaysia, the Philippines, Brunei, and Taiwan also claim all or part of the Spratly Islands. Over the years, conflicting claims have produced small-scale armed altercations in the area; in 1988, 70 Vietnamese sailors died in a confrontation with China in the Spratlys. China's assertion of "indisputable sovereignty" over the Spratly Islands and the entire South China Sea has elicited concern from Vietnam and its Southeast Asia neighbors. Tensions escalated in the latter half of 2007 as, according to press reports, China pressured foreign oil companies to abandon their oil and gas exploration contracts with Vietnam in the South China Sea. Vietnamese students staged several anti-China demonstrations in response, prompting a warning from the Chinese Foreign Ministry spokesman that Hanoi's failure to quell the demonstrations was harming relations. China's efforts in the summer of 2009 to strictly enforce its unilateral fishing ban in disputed waters led to the detention for several weeks of more than two dozen Vietnamese fishermen.

In contrast, Vietnam has made significant progress with China in delineating its northern land border and the Gulf of Tonkin, pursuant to a Land Border Agreement signed in December 1999, and an Agreement on Borders in the Gulf of Tonkin signed in December 2000. The two sides completed demarcation of their land border in December 2008 and have reached understanding on maritime boundaries in the mouth of the Tonkin Gulf.

US-Vietnam Relations

President Bill Clinton announced the formal normalization of diplomatic relations with the Socialist Republic of Vietnam on July 11, 1995. Subsequent to President Clinton's normalization announcement, in August 1995, both nations upgraded their Liaison Offices opened in January 1995 to embassy status. As diplomatic ties between the nations grew, the United States opened a consulate general in Ho Chi Minh City, and Vietnam opened a consulate general in San Francisco. In 2009, the United States received permission to open a consulate in Danang; in 2010, Vietnam officially inaugurated a consulate general in Houston.

US relations with Vietnam have become increasingly cooperative and broad-based in the years since political normalization. A series of bilateral summits have helped drive the improvement of ties, including President George W. Bush's visit to Hanoi in November 2006, President Triet's visit to Washington in June 2007, Prime Minister Dung's visits to Washington in June 2008 and April 2010, and President Truong Tan Sang's visit to Hawaii for APEC meetings in November 2011. The two countries hold an annual dialogue on human rights, which resumed in 2006 after a 2-year hiatus. Vietnam and the United States signed a Bilateral Trade Agreement in July 2000, which went into force in December 2001. In 2003, the two countries signed a Counternarcotics Letter of Agreement (amended in 2006), a Civil Aviation Agreement (amended in 2008), and a textile agreement. In December 2006 the United States granted permanent normal trade relations (PNTR) to Vietnam. In October 2008, the US and Vietnam inaugurated annual political-military talks and policy planning talks to consult on regional security and strategic issues. In August 2010, the US Department of Defense and Vietnam's Ministry of Defense held the first round of annual high-level defense talks, known as the Defense Policy Dialogue. Bilateral and regional diplomatic engagement has expanded at ASEAN, which Vietnam chaired in 2010, and continues through APEC.

Vietnam's suppression of political dissent has continued to be a main issue of contention in relations with the United States, drawing criticism from successive administrations, as well as from members of Congress and the US public. Within the previous 2 years, Vietnam's government has convicted more than 22 political dissidents, and has arrested an additional 15 others. The government has continued to further tighten controls over the Internet, press, and freedom of speech. Internet bloggers were also arrested, jailed, and convicted after writing about corruption, and protesting China's actions in the disputed Spratly and Paracel Islands and Chinese mining of bauxite in the central highlands.

In contrast, Vietnam has continued to make progress on expanding religious freedom, although significant issues remain. In 2005, Vietnam passed comprehensive religious freedom legislation, outlawing forced renunciations and permitting the official recognition of new denominations. Since that time, the government has granted official national recognition or registration to a number of new religions and religious groups, including eight more Protestant denominations, and has registered hundreds of local congregations particularly in the central highlands. As a result, in November 2006, the Department of State lifted the designation of Vietnam as a "Country of Particular Concern," based on a determination that the country was no longer a serious violator of religious freedoms, as defined by the International Religious Freedom Act. The Department of State has reaffirmed this decision every year since then. Nevertheless, there is room for further progress. The government's slow pace of church registration, particularly in the northwest highlands, and harassment of certain religious leaders for their political activism, remain an ongoing source of US concern.

As of November 2011, the US Government listed 1,679 Americans unaccounted for in Southeast Asia, including 1,288 in Vietnam. Since 1973, 967 Americans have been accounted for, including 683 in Vietnam. Additionally, the Department of Defense has confirmed that of the 196 individuals who were "last known alive" (LKA) in Vietnam, the US Government has determined the fate of all but 25. The Joint POW/MIA Accounting command (JPAC) conducts four major investigation and recovery periods a year in Vietnam, during which specially trained US military and civilian personnel investigate and excavate hundreds of cases in pursuit of the fullest possible accounting. Unrestricting areas previously denied to JPAC personnel has been a recent highlight of cooperation by the Socialist Republic of Vietnam, as was the first-ever turnover of POW/MIA-related artifacts from the Vietnam Military History Museum, apparently a reciprocal action in response to US turnovers of Vietnamese war artifacts. In June 2009, a coastal search mission by the oceanographic survey ship USNS Heezen was the first of its kind, creating the potential to recover hundreds of underwater crash sites. The US would still like to see the provision of archival documents related to US losses along the wartime Ho Chi Minh Trail, as well as more openness in general with regard to Vietnam's wartime archives. The United States considers achieving the fullest possible accounting of Americans missing and unaccounted for in Indochina to be one of its highest priorities with Vietnam.

Since entry into force of the US-Vietnam Bilateral Trade Agreement on December 10, 2001, increased trade between the US and Vietnam, combined with large-scale US investment in Vietnam, evidence the maturing US-Vietnam economic relationship. In 2010, the United States exported $3.7 billion in goods to Vietnam and imported $14.9 billion in goods from Vietnam. Similarly, US companies continue to invest directly in the Vietnamese economy. During 2009, the US private sector committed $9.8 billion to Vietnam in foreign direct investment. Another sign of the expanding bilateral relationship is the signing of a Bilateral Air Transport Agreement in December 2003. Several US carriers already have third-party code sharing agreements with Vietnam Airlines. Direct flights between Ho Chi Minh City and San Francisco began in December 2004. The Bilateral Air Transport Agreement was amended in October 2008 to fully open markets for cargo air transportation. Vietnam and the United States also signed a Bilateral Maritime Agreement in March 2007 that opened the maritime transport and services industry of Vietnam to US firms.

Vietnam remains heavily contaminated by explosive remnants of war, primarily in the form of unexploded ordnance (UXO) including extensive contamination by cluster munitions dating from the war with the United States. The United States is the largest single donor to UXO/mine action. The Department of State continues to assist Vietnam in detecting and clearing unexploded ordnance, educating the public on the risks of UXO, and providing assistance to the victims of UXO. Since 1993, US has contributed over $62 million in UXO clearance, risk education, and victims' assistance programs and support for persons with disabilities, regardless of cause.

While legacy issues such as UXO/demining, MIA accounting, and Agent Orange provided the foundations for the US-Vietnam defense relationship, mutual interest in addressing the challenges of humanitarian assistance/disaster relief, search and rescue, and maritime security have allowed the defense relationship to accelerate in the past 3 years, with Vietnam participating in US-provided capacity-building training in these areas. Many of these topics are discussed in annual bilateral defense discussions. In August 2010, a delegation of senior Vietnamese civilian and military officials participated in a fly-out to the USS George Washington in international waters off the coast of Vietnam just prior to the USS John S. McCain visit to Danang, Vietnam. In July 2011 another delegation of government and military officials participated in a fly-out and tour aboard the USS George Washington.

Two years after its first visit to Vietnam, the hospital ship USNS Mercy paid a port call to Quy Nhon in June 2010, where it provided medical and dental treatment to thousands; the USNS Mercy's June 2008 visit to Nha Trang reached over 11,000 Vietnamese patients. Other US Navy visits in 2011 included the first US military ship visit to Cam Ranh Bay in over three decades, when the USNS Richard E. Byrd entered the port for maintenance and repair in August 2011; the USNS Diehl followed for routine maintenance and repair in October. Vietnam continues to observe multinational exercises such as the Cooperation Afloat Readiness and Training (CARAT) organized by the US Pacific Fleet and the yearly GPOI CAPSTONE exercise organized by the US Pacific Command. An active partner in nonproliferation regimes, Vietnam also takes full advantage of expertise, equipment, and training available under the Export Control and Related Border Security (EXBS) program. With the support of the US Department of Energy's Megaports Initiative, Vietnam is installing radiation detection equipment to help it detect and identify weapons of mass destruction and their components at the commercial port of Cai Mep-Vung Tau. Vietnam agreed in 2010 to join the Global Initiative to Combat Nuclear Terrorism, and Prime Minister Dung was an active participant in President Barack Obama's April 2010 Nuclear Security Summit in Washington.

INDEX

D

E

F

G

H

I

J

K

L

M

N

O

P

Q

R

S

T